FISCAL POLICY AND BUSINESS CAPITAL FORMATION

A SYMPOSIUM SPONSORED BY
THE AMERICAN ENTERPRISE INSTITUTE
FOR PUBLIC POLICY RESEARCH
WASHINGTON, D. C.

iii

iv

Foreword

This volume contains the proceedings of a symposium held in Washington, D. C., in April, 1967, by the American Enterprise Institute for Public Policy Research. The Institute's purpose in organizing the symposium was to present a responsible discussion of an important national-policy matter.

Those who took part in the discussions were of recognized and demonstrated competence in the areas of fiscal policy, business capital spending, and investment decision making. None, however, spoke from an official position. Thus, it was hoped, the discussion of issues would be as wide-ranging as possible.

The symposium explored capital investment from the standpoint of the business executive and government tax and fiscal policy as it affects business executives' decisions on investments. Current views on tax adjustments and a review of the postwar experience in administering fiscal policy, together with comments on some of the politics of policymaking, were presented by various participants. Objectives of fiscal and budget policies and the proper blending of fiscal and monetary policies were also discussed.

In addition to those persons appearing on the program, some 250 guests, representing the corporate and academic communities, attended. Observers from the legislative and executive branches of government also were present.

This volume is organized in three parts, each of which covers the major papers, the comments of discussants, and the questions and statements from the floor of one half-day session of the symposium.

THOMAS F. JOHNSON, *Director of Research*
American Enterprise Institute for Public Policy Research

October, 1967

v

BIOGRAPHICAL NOTES
ON AUTHORS AND DISCUSSANTS

WILLIAM J. BAUMOL

Professor of Economics, Princeton University.

Member, Council of Economic Advisers to Governor of New Jersey, 1966.

Vice President, American Economic Association, 1966-67.

Director of Economic Analysis, MATHEMATICA, Inc., Princeton.

Economist and Consultant, U.S. Department of Agriculture, 1942-43, 1946, 1951.

Publications include: *Economic Dynamics* (1961, 1959); *Welfare Economics and the Theory of the State* (1952); *Business Behavior, Value and Growth* (1959, 1967); *Economic Theory and Operations Analysis* (1961, 1966); *The Stock Market and Economic Efficiency* (1965); *Performing Arts: The Economic Dilemma* (with W. G. Bowen, 1966).

HAROLD BIERMAN, JR.

Professor of Accounting and Managerial Economics, Graduate School of Business and Public Administration, Cornell University.

Business Consultant, including Hooker Chemical Corporation, Boeing Airplane Company, Ford Motor Company.

vii

Publications include: *Financial and Managerial Accounting; The Capital Budgeting Decision; Quantitative Analysis for Business Decision; Topics in Cost Accounting.*

SOLOMON FABRICANT

Professor of Economics, New York University, and Member of Research Staff, National Bureau of Economic Research.

Director of Research, National Bureau of Economic Research, 1954-65. Economic Consultant to numerous government agencies.

Chairman, Executive Committee, Conference on Research in Income and Wealth, 1949-51.

Chairman, Research Advisory Board, Committee for Economic Development, 1960-61.

Vice President, American Economic Association, 1960-61.

Publications include: *Measurement of Technological Change* (1965); *Towards a Firmer Basis of Economic Policy* (1961); *A Respect for Facts* (1960); *Basic Facts on Productivity Change* (1959); *The Study of Economic Growth* (1959); *Investing in Economic Knowledge* (1958); *Economic Progress and Economic Change* (1954).

WILLIAM J. FELLNER

Sterling Professor of Economics, Yale University.

Member of the OECD's Committee of Independent Experts on the problem of rising prices and joint author of committee report.

Member of international study group of thirty-two economists on the problems of international monetary arrangements which issued its report in 1964.

Publications include: *Competition Among the Few* (1949); *Trends and Cycles in Economic Activity* (1956); *Emergence and Content of Modern Economic Analysis* (1960); *Probability and Profit* (1965).

GOTTFRIED HABERLER

Galen L. Stone Professor of International Trade, Harvard University.

Member of Academic Advisory Board, American Enterprise Institute.

Director, National Bureau of Economic Research.

President, American Economic Association, 1963.

President of the International Economic Association, 1950-53; now honorary president.

Economist, Board of Governors, Federal Reserve System, 1943-47.

Expert, Financial Section, League of Nations, 1934-36.

Professor of Economics, University of Vienna, 1928-36.

Publications include: *Prosperity and Depression* (1942); *Quantitative Trade Controls, their Causes and Nature* (1943).

C. LOWELL HARRISS

Professor of Economics, Columbia University.

Member of Academic Advisory Board, American Enterprise
  Institute.
Economic Consultant, Tax Foundation, Inc.
Economic Consultant to numerous government agencies.
Vice President, Tax Institute of America.
Director, International Institute of Public Finance.
Former president, Metropolitan (New York City) Economic
  Association.
Fulbright Professor. Netherlands School of Economics, Rot-
  terdam, and University of Strasbourg, France.
Publications include: *Gift Taxation in the United States;
American Public Finance* (with W. J. Schultz, Inc., 8th edi-
tion, 1965); *The American Economy* (5th edition, 1965);
Selected Readings in Economics (2d edition, 1962); *History
and Policies of the Home Owners Loan Corporation; Money
and Banking* (2d edition, 1965); *Economics* (with Good-
man, 1963).

WILLIAM T. HOGAN

*Professor of Economics, Fordham Uni-
versity.*

Director, Fordham University Industrial Economics Program.

Inaugurated Industrial Economics Program at Fordham.

Publications include: *Productivity in the Blast Furnace and
Open Hearth Segments of the Steel Industry; The Development of American Heavy Industry in the Twentieth Century; Depreciation Policies and Resultant Problems; The
History and Economics of the Iron and Steel Industry.*

PAUL W. McCRACKEN

Edmund Ezra Day University Professor of Business Administration, University of Michigan.

Chairman of Academic Advisory Board, American Enterprise Institute.

Member of the President's Council of Economic Advisers, 1956-58.

Federal Reserve Bank of Minneapolis, Financial Economist, 1943-45; Director of Research, 1945-48.

Economist, U.S. Department of Commerce, 1942-43.

Publications include: *Price Level Stability for or vs. Growth* (1961); *The Balance of Payments and Domestic Prosperity* (1963); *Basic Sources of Our Economic Growth* (1963).

ALLAN H. MELTZER

Professor of Economics, Carnegie Institute of Technology, Graduate School of Industrial Administration.

Ford Foundation Visiting Professor, Department of Economics, University of Chicago, 1964-65.

Ford Faculty Research Fellow, 1962-63.

Fellow, Social Science Research Council and Fulbright scholar in France, 1955-56.

Publications include: *An Analysis of Federal Reserve Monetary Policymaking*, Banking and Currency Committee (with Karl Brunner, 1964); *The Taxation of Income from State*

and Local Government Securities (with David Ott, 1963);
A Study of the Dealer Market for U.S. Government Securities, Joint Economic Committee (with G. von der Linde, 1960).

RICHARD A. MUSGRAVE

Professor of Economics, Harvard University.

Consultant, United States Treasury Department, Council of Economic Advisers, and the Department of Housing and Urban Development.

Professor of Economics, University of Michigan, Johns Hopkins, Princeton, 1948-65.

Former Vice President, American Economic Association.

Consultant, United Nations and Harvard Tax Mission to Chile.

Economist, Board of Governors, Federal Reserve System, late 1940s.

Publications include: *Theory of Public Finance.*

CARL S. SHOUP

Professor of Economics, Columbia University.

Director of Fiscal Survey of Venezuela, 1958.
President, International Institute of Public Finance, 1950-53.
Co-director, New York City Finance Study, 1950-52.
Director, Shoup Tax Mission to Japan, 1949-50.
Twentieth Century Fund Survey of Taxation in the United

States, 1935-37.

Publications include: *Fiscal Harmonization in Common Markets*, Editor (1966); *Ricardo on Taxation* (1960); *The Fiscal System of Venezuela* (1959); *Principles of National Income Analysis* (1947).

DAN THROOP SMITH

Professor of Finance, Harvard University.

Chairman of the Board, Fisons Corporation.

Consultant, Brookings Institution, National Bureau of Economic Research, and Committee for Economic Development.

Deputy to the Secretary of Treasury, 1957-59; Special Assistant to the Secretary, 1955-57; Assistant to the Secretary, 1953-55.

Director, Army-Air Force Statistical School, 1943-45.

Publications include: *Federal Tax Reform—the Issues and a Program* (1961); *Effects of Taxation—Corporate Financial Policy* (1952); *Taxable and Business Income* (with J. K. Butters, 1949); *Deficits and Depressions* (1936).

ARTHUR SMITHIES

Nathaniel Ropes Professor of Political Economy, Harvard University.

Editor, *Journal of Economic Statistics*, 1965-
Master of Kirkland House, Harvard University, 1965-
Editor, *Quarterly Journal of Economics*, 1957-65.

Visiting Professor, Australian National University, 1962; Oxford University, 1955-56.

Economic Consultant to numerous government agencies.

Publications include: *Coordination of Monetary and Fiscal Policy* (forthcoming, 1967); "The Effect Abroad of American Private Enterprise," *Annals of the American Academy of Political and Social Science* (1966); "A Conceptual Framework for the Program Budget," *Program Budgeting*, RAND Corporation (1965); *Government Decision-Making and the Theory of Choice*, RAND Corporation (1964); "Inflation in Latin America," *Public Policy* (1964); *Economic Stabilization in Australia* (1963); "Australian Economic Strategy," *Economic Record* (1963).

ROBERT W. STONE

Senior Vice President, National Bank of Detroit.

Vice President, Federal Reserve Bank of New York; Manager, Federal Reserve System Open Market Account, 1962-65.

Economist, Federal Reserve Bank of New York, 1953-58.

NORMAN B. TURE

Director of Tax Studies, National Bureau of Economic Research.

Economist, Joint Economic Committee, United States Congress.

Fiscal Economist, Analysis staff, Tax Division, Office of the Secretary of the Treasury.

Publications include: *Accelerated Depreciation in the United States* (1954-60) ; "Tax Reform Depreciation Problems," *Papers and Proceedings of the American Economic Association. 75th Annual Meeting* (1963); "Distribution of Tax Reductions," *Proceedings of 56th Annual Conference on Taxation,* National Tax Association (1953); "Growth Aspects of Federal Tax Policy," *Journal of Finance* (May, 1962); "Tax Reform for Growth and Stability," *Tax Reform: Why and How?, Proceedings of the 3rd 1961 Economic Institute,* Chamber of Commerce of the United States (1961).

R. C. TYSON

Chairman, Finance Committee, United States Steel Corporation.

Member, Board of Directors, United States Steel Corporation.

Member of the Advisory Board, The Hoover Institution on War, Revolution, and Peace, Stanford University.

Vice President, member of the Board of Directors, and Executive Committee, Commerce and Industry Association of New York.

Vice President, New York Chamber of Commerce.

Chairman, Tax Foundation.

Trustee, Princeton University.

Director, Boys' Clubs of America.

Trustee, Virginia Foundation for Independent Colleges.

Trustee, American Enterprise Institute.

HENRY C. WALLICH

Professor of Economics, Yale University.

Member of President's Council of Economic Advisers, 1959-60.

Special Assistant, U.S. Secretary of the Treasury, 1958-60.

Director, Foreign Research Division, Federal Reserve Bank of New York, 1946-51; Economist, 1941-51.

Chief, Intra-European Payments Branch, Economic Cooperation Administration, 1948.

Consultant, Gordon Gray Group Report to the President on Foreign Economic Policies, 1950.

Financial Consultant, Special Mission of the Economic Cooperation Administration to Portugal.

Publications include: *Mainsprings of the German Revival* (1955); *The Cost of Freedom* (1960).

CONTENTS

PART III:

PART I

BUSINESS CAPITAL SPENDING AND INVESTMENT DECISIONS

ROBERT C. TYSON

UCH PUBLIC attention is currently being given to the question of the appropriate fiscal policy for today's —and tomorrow's—economy. This symposium should materially aid in the evaluation of various fiscal alternatives, but I believe it can also have longer-range value by creating an improved public understanding of the crucial role of expanding capital investment for progress in our free competitive enterprise economy. I would like to discuss three areas: First, the crucial role of expanding capital investment; second, some of the factors within an organization which have an important bearing on business capital spending and investment decisions; and third, some of the factors which determine the general climate for investment.

The Crucial Role of Capital Investment*

In examining the crucial role of expanding capital investment for growth in our free competitive enterprise economy, there are certain points which, in my judgment, cannot be emphasized too often. In any competitive enterprise economy

---

*This subject is discussed more fully in U.S. Steel's Annual Report for 1966, pages 32-38.

1

there is one and only one way in which new, productive, self-sustaining jobs come into existence: It is by the investment of savings in plant and equipment—the tools of production—which men operate in order to produce the marketable values to cover their continuing wages and the catalyst of those wages —the investors' profits. Profits mean tools; tools mean jobs. Tools have not replaced labor; rather, new jobs have replaced old jobs. Today's tools realign and expand job opportunities.

During the next decade the total labor force in this country is expected to grow from its present level of about 80 million to about 95 million. Thus, new capital will have to be provided for each of these new jobs. In addition, old jobs will have to be "recapitalized" to reflect new technologies. It follows that the greater a nation's technological attainment, the greater is its dependence on capital in relation to labor—that is, the more capital required for each job. It also follows that in a private enterprise economy such as ours, economic progress and human progress require continually expanding investment in the tools of production; continually expanding investment requires continually expanding savings. One key way to save more, apart from consuming less, is to earn more—to produce more income.

But production of more income requires more and better tools to equip a growing labor force. In this way, there is more production of better goods and services, in greater variety, at lower cost, to satisfy more consumers. Consumers can then consume more and can save, lend, and invest more.

Through their savings, consumers provide more capital funds and, through their purchases, more sales revenues. These revenues in turn provide the return *of* investment, in the form of depreciation. Hopefully, they also provide something more: a return *on* investment risked, in the form of profit. Part of this profit may be saved by the business firm and reinvested in plant and equipment; part may be paid to investors, which they in turn may reinvest or consume.

Increasing the supply of jobs and the output of today's and tomorrow's employees and increasing their productivity requires improvement in the quality and quantity of capital goods. These increases depend upon adequate recognition and compensation of *both* labor and capital. Thus, capital's key contribution to the supply of jobs and to increasing productivity depends upon the incentive to increase investment in productive capacity and in new technology.

Only a few months ago, however, questions were being raised about the rate of investment in plant and equipment; there was debate about inflation and whether it was caused by what some called an excessively high level of capital spending. It is my view that the vigorous year-to-year increases in capital expenditures since the early 1960s—in large part, reflecting a "catching up" process—were a capital goods boon rather than boom. If inflation is too much money chasing too *few* goods, then capital expenditures in the short run, like all other expenditures, can add to inflationary pressures. But in the long run, since they facilitate more production and hence *more* goods, they perform an anti-inflationary role, and so should be the last type of expenditure to be curtailed.

This is not to say that some inflation has not occurred, but rather to question whether or not the occurrence can be traced to capital spending. In answering this question, I believe it is pertinent to compare trends in the cost of labor with those for the cost of the tools of production. A review of the components of price indices and of their movements leads me to the conclusion that in the private economy the rate of increase in the cost of an hour's work has been significantly greater than that for the cost of a unit of the capital equipment from which improvements in output and efficiency mainly come. In other words, tools in 1966 were in effect cheaper relative to wages than they were in the 1957-59 period. This capital cost advantage, a trend which I believe will continue, reinforces the anti-inflationary role of investment.

A final point about the crucial role of capital investment in our economy—one which is more widely recognized but too often forgotten: A continuing high level of investment makes possible a higher standard of living than would otherwise be possible and also permits our nation to more ably defend the freedoms which we all cherish so highly.

Capital Investment Factors Within the Firm

Turning now to my second area of discussion, I want to examine with you some of the factors within an organization which importantly bear on the business decisions of when, where, how, why, and what a company invests in plant and equipment—decisions which critically determine its long- and short-term economic future.

Business firms make investments in plant and equipment only when there is an adequate incentive—either the hope of profit from doing so or the fear of loss from not doing so. When the prospect of profit is sufficient to compensate for the use and risk of the money required, companies will eagerly invest in the tools of production and hire people to utilize those tools. When this prospect dims, there will be a lower level of investment, which in turn breeds unemployment and economic slowdown. And when this prospect is eliminated, new investment will tend to come to a standstill.

This principle has long been recognized by economists. For example, the late Lord Keynes in analyzing the unsatisfactory economic condition of his own country in 1931 wrote:

We live in a society organized in such a way that the activity of production depends on the individual businessman hoping for a reasonable profit, or at least, to avoid an actual loss. The margin which he requires as his necessary incentive to produce may be a very small proportion of the total value of the product. But take this away from him and the whole process stops. This, unluckily, is just what has happened. The fall of prices relative to costs, together with the psychological effect of high taxation, has destroyed the necessary incentive to production.

Perhaps not too surprisingly, then, a close relationship exists in our economy between capital expenditures and corporate profits. When profits as a percent of gross national product are high, so too are capital expenditures; when profits are low, capital expenditures are likewise low. All peacetime years for which records are available and in which production and employment have been regarded as significantly above normal have been years in which profits were greater than average. All years regarded as depression years have been years in which profits have been smaller or replaced by losses. So, profits and prospective profits are crucial incentives.

Prospective profits reflect expected revenues and costs. As to revenues, under our competitive enterprise system prices can only be determined in the marketplace. Any other price controls dampen materially the incentive to invest. As to costs, the most significant item for business is related to employment, directly or indirectly. Employment costs, too, should be fairly and competitively determined with equal strength on each side of the bargaining table. Given these conditions of competitively determined prices and wages, prospective profits will also be fairly and competitively determined—thus maximizing total investment in job-creating, job-sustaining tools of production and also, incidentally, maximizing government revenues. Given the conditions of controlled prices or wages or both, the system goes awry.

I would like to turn now to some specific considerations underlying proposed investments in plant and equipment. Assuming a company has developed a sound business objective, the planning of a broad investment program should start with projections of the future, the uncertainties of which increase as one projects further away from the present. When the plan involves, for example, the building of a new plant or the transfer of a major development from the laboratory to commercial production, some of the necessary projections cover: the general growth rate of the economy, expected growth of general and specific markets, potential new markets, competitive actions by other producers, competition from other materials, and the company's prospective share in markets. Other projections must evaluate the impact of advancing technology, the adaptability of this equipment to change, and—all-importantly—the proper timing of such expenditure. Obviously, the longer the period covered by such projections, the greater the uncertainty, and the greater the difficulty in assessing the relative risks and the opportunities for profit.

When the proposed capital expenditure project is concerned solely with the replacement of existing facilities, the problem is essentially one of ascertaining whether from a physical or operating standpoint the function needs to be continued and, if so, determining what type, size, timing, and location of equipment will most economically perform the required function. From these initial planning steps there generally results a long list of desired projects without full regard for expected profitability or the amount of funds which may be available.

The financial evaluation of the plan involves projecting revenues over part or all of the expected period of economic life of the facilities, determining the expected costs and benefits for the same period, comparing these benefits in some manner with the required capital outlay, examining the probabilities of possible alternative outcomes, ranking the projects in some order of priority, and finally deciding how many projects to undertake in light of known circumstances, including availability of funds and cost of financing.

The plan for each item of the investment program must be integrated and coordinated with existing facilities as well as with plans for other future facilities. Since the program generally calls for expenditures against specific items over a period of years, it must be sufficiently flexible to accommodate changes which may occur.

I believe you would agree that capital expenditure planning is neither simple nor certain; it merely represents the combined best judgment of many skilled people about variables with respect to markets, technology, prices, costs, and many other factors. I would also emphasize that any resultant numbers expressed in such terms as rate of return, payback period, or net present value are no better than the underlying assumptions on which they are based. Indeed, the many decisions necessary just to arrive at all these underlying assumptions increase the complexities, hazards, and risks of capital investment planning.

At this point, I feel that another observation is in order. Literature on investment planning seems to place relatively more emphasis on the purely mathematical aspects of the problem rather than on recognition that mathematics only quantifies many factors involved in sound business judgment. Mathematics, however, can never replace the decision maker although it can improve the odds that the decision will be a good one.

With all this, the application of good business judgment, however, does not insure that all investment decisions will be right because no one has perfect foresight. Some investments may turn out better than expected; others, as expected; and still others, worse than expected.

After a long-range or broad facility program has been formulated, each component part must again be reviewed prior to authorization of actual construction. The many factors previously considered must be re-evaluated so as to reflect any changed conditions. This updating is most important in reaching a final judgment.

In capital expenditure decisions, as in many other areas, hindsight tells us our mistakes. Capital expenditure decisions, however, are based upon circumstances known or anticipated before the fact. Thus, it is only in the light of those circumstances that valid conclusions can later be drawn with respect to the soundness of previous investment judgments.

How Much Can We Sell?

I now would like to discuss product demand. Present and future levels of demand significantly affect the timing, nature, and amount of capital investments. The first consideration for any company is one of adequately and economically meeting present demand, for a company which fails to meet this demand runs the risk of losing customers—temporarily or permanently—to competitors who can supply current needs; such a company also diminishes its ability to attract new customers. Thus, short-term investment planning for most industrial companies involves weighing the cost of having capacity somewhat in excess of normal demand against the probable cost of overtime production, extra shift operations, and other expedients. For industries which are subject to wide variations in demand, it necessarily means building some capacity to take care of peak demand. This is why during periods of less than peak demand, capacity appears to be "excessive."

Meeting longer-term demand requires, among other things, a forecast of the prospective demand for products by specific markets over the near-term and longer-term future; determination of the time when the production will be needed and the time which would be required to build the additional facilities and to develop and to penetrate the market; an educated guess about prospective actions and reactions of competitors offering similar or substitute products; and an evaluation of the prospective profitability from satisfying this demand.

From all this, the key judgment is made by selecting the best alternative—whether to dispose of an existing facility, to replace it, to modernize it, or to add entirely new facilities. If an unusually high level of demand for one or more products is expected only over the near-term future, attention would undoubtedly be focused on modernizing existing facilities rather than replacing old facilities or adding new. This is so because such modernization can usually be effected speedily and with minimum cost and risk. This approach, of course, assumes that existing equipment is relatively efficient and thus not in need of immediate replacement.

The following example of demand considerations and the related investment response, while related to the steel industry, is also applicable to both large and small firms in other industries. From the end of World War II through the mid-1950s, the demand for steel was far above that of any sustained long-term experience and was expanding rapidly. Satisfying this demand solely by means of building new steelmaking facilities did not appear practical because of the extended period required for the construction, and the vast sums needed for such a program at a time when considerable doubt existed that such a growth rate could continue. Additional steelmaking capacity was obtained quickly, however, by innovative investment to obtain greater production from existing steelmaking facilities. Some innovative examples include the installation of more efficient materials handling equipment, which speeded up the input of materials into the steelmaking furnaces; the installation of oxygen injection equipment, which permitted faster melting and refining of the materials (an accomplishment possible only after the development of furnace brick and furnace designs which would withstand the higher temperatures); and the development and installation of sensitive control devices, which minimized the time involved in making human judgments. The increase in steelmaking capacity from those and other efforts was substantial; it was also accomplished at a minimum capital cost.

In hindsight, however, some have contended that the investment instead should have been in a new process which was in its infant stage of development in the late 1940s, in limited small-scale production by the mid-fifties, and not generally economical for mass production by American standards until the

1960s. The new process now is being used extensively. Had we scrapped existing steelmaking facilities in the early 1950s in favor of this new process—rather than maximizing the productivity from existing furnaces—then we really would have invested in the wrong kind of capacity.

There was a different response starting in the latter part of 1957 as the demand for steel dropped sharply and remained at a low level for some five years. In fact, during the early 1960s many individuals were predicting that there was little prospect of any significant increase in steel demand. During this period of below normal demand and with no immediate increase foreseeable, capital expenditures were directed primarily toward the improvement of finishing equipment to provide the greater variety, flexibility, and quality demanded by customers and to other projects aimed at holding existing customers and attracting new ones. These expenditures enhanced the ability to gain incremental units of production. A small increase in volume generated a more than proportional improvement in profit. Simultaneously, there was also a marked increase in research activity aimed at developing new production in processes and new products for the marketplace.

During the most recent five-year period, steel production and consumption have increased dramatically. Expenditures for plant and equipment have also expanded rapidly, with major facility investments having been made to incorporate the many recent process improvements to produce products more efficiently and with better quality, and also to produce the many new products that have recently been developed.

These demand-related factors I have discussed are, of course, only some of those which bear on capital investment decisions.

What About Competitive Actions and Reactions?

There are always competitive responses to investment decisions. Every firm competes for equipment superiority, hopefully to gain a cost or market advantage and a profit advantage. Market advantage can come from such things as developing and acquiring equipment for the manufacture of new products and equipment for upgrading product quality and utility. It can also come from invention and development of new processes, as well as from providing better customer service and, hopefully, more sales for one's own products through building new markets for customers' products.

But competitors react to a company's investment actions and in turn seek to gain a competitive advantage. Certain of the company's decisions will necessarily be in reaction to these competitive moves. Other decisions by a company will have a competitive impact on other products which it produces. The investment action taken will, of course, depend on all of the pertinent facts and circumstances facing each situation; when these facts and circumstances are different, there is justification for different actions—each thought best suited to the individual needs of the individual company. Let me briefly describe two examples of competitive actions and reactions which have taken place in the past few years.

Tin mill products—light steel sheets, electrolytically coated with an extremely thin layer of tin—have changed dramatically over the years. About seven years ago, a new process was developed—through research—for the production of a new product called "thin tin"; this product resulted in large part because of the intense market competition from glass, paper, fibres, plastics, and other materials. By the new process the steel sheet could be so reduced in thickness that for many uses some 30 to 40 percent more containers could be formed from the same weight of steel—a saving to the customer, a boon to steel, and possibly some capturing of markets from other materials. Today, following further developments, the steel sheet can be reduced to the thinness of a sheet of fine paper—steel foil. These and other developments in turn have opened up other markets and have forced competitive investment by many producers. One interesting reaction already has been the development of products using steel foil in combination with other materials. Undoubtedly, there will be further reaction.

Another example concerns the installation of a new extra-wide plate mill to replace one existing mill, to complement other existing mills, and to expand production to meet a large and growing market for this plate product. This new mill can produce about 3.5 times as much product as the replaced mill could produce when it was originally built; however, because of improvements which had been made to it over the years, the original capacity of the old mill had been more than doubled by the time it was replaced. This dramatically illustrates the continuing refinements and improvements that are made to plant and equipment and the eternal effort to remain competitive.

An interesting situation has been created by this investment. The product of this new mill is twice as wide as the product from one of the existing mills it complements and also wider than any other product previously available. Prior to the construction of this mill, customers who needed extra wide plates purchased two of the narrower plates and welded them together. If the price for the new wider product is economically attractive, customers will change their purchasing pattern and eliminate their welding operation. In this way the productive capacity of the new unit will be utilized but this, in turn, creates a problem of disposing of the product from the narrower mills.

Thus, actions of competitors and the forces of competition are clearly prime movers in any company's investment decisions. The manner in which these actions are met depends again on the particular facts and circumstances facing each company.

What Are the Risks Involved?

I would now like to discuss some other types of risk. Consider the risk that exists when a decision is made to invest millions of dollars in a revolutionary, thoroughly research-tested, but commercially untried process. Until a full-scale commercial installation becomes operative, there are always unresolved questions. For example, is production really possible on a large-scale basis? Will the equipment produce a full range of commercially acceptable products? Will the customer buy and keep buying? Will the actual capacity of the new facilities be sufficient for an economic process? Will the operating cost be within the projection? Will there be a satisfactory profit margin?

A steel industry case in point is continuous casting. The concept of continuous casting of steel directly from molten metal to an in-process product has been known for over a hundred years, but active development, testing, and some limited commercial use has occurred only in the last decade. The casting process eliminates many present operations and, if large-scale production is achieved, promises to involve less capital investment and be lower in operating cost than conventional methods. To date the few commercial installations have been in small-scale operations, because of the limited range of products and grades for which commercial capabilities have been proven.

U. S. Steel's research people have been actively studying continuous casting for more than ten years. A large pilot unit has been in operation for some five years, new grades of steel have been developed for this process, and steel has been cast and converted into finished steel products which have been tested in commercial applications. In 1964, U. S. Steel initiated construction of a commercial-size, high capacity, versatile, continuous casting unit. By mid-year we expect to have this unit in operation as part of a vast new production complex. In this complex, steel from new basic oxygen furnaces will continuously feed the casting unit, which will produce superior quality slabs up to 76 inches wide in a continuous strand. The strand will be cut into desired lengths of slabs to be converted on a new completely automated hot strip mill into huge coils of sheet steel.

At the time construction of this casting facility was authorized, we believed that a full range of slab steels could be produced satisfactorily on such a unit; that the finished product would be commercially acceptable; and that the productive capacity and operating costs would be superior to those obtainable from a modern but conventional slab rolling mill. But we didn't know for sure. These were some of the risks we assumed. While a slab casting unit as large as this has never been built anywhere else in the world, we were and are convinced that the opportunity to gain a competitive advantage and to realize an improvement in profit merit the risk. We believe this installation can revolutionize steel processing techniques, just as did the continuous hot strip mill introduced during the 1930s.

Technological obsolescence is another form of risk. Except for brief moments in time, it is unlikely that any company—

even a new one—has all of the most modern processes and techniques. So there is always some degree of obsolescence. With new production processes, it is common for improvements to occur frequently during the early years of their operation. It does not follow, however, that a new process will necessarily eliminate existing competitive processes immediately; in fact, such a happening is a rare occurrence in industry.

The production of steel in basic oxygen furnaces versus in conventional open hearth furnaces is an excellent example. The basic oxygen process, first introduced in Europe in the early 1950s, was adopted by some producers in the United States in the mid and late 1950s. It was not widely adopted until later. For those producers who needed to replace worn-out equipment, or who needed to add steelmaking furnaces to gain capacity, there was an economic advantage both in capital cost and in operating cost in installing the new-type units as against building new open hearth shops. Early installations, however, ran a great risk of technological obsolescence, and some are already being retired. Other producers who were not faced with the need for replacement, or who had obtained adequate capacity by minimum investment additions to existing equipment, waited because for them it was advantageous economically to utilize existing modern open hearth furnaces which could produce competitive product at competitive cost.

Could We Use the Money Better Somewhere Else?

Undoubtedly, the opportunity for plant and equipment expenditures within most companies greatly exceeds the supply of available funds—the economists' concept of opportunity cost is always present. It follows that there must be an allocation of funds among the prospective projects—for example, first to those that are required by law, contract, or public policy and then on some priority basis recognizing commercial or production necessity, commercial desirability, efficiency improvements, and other factors.

The techniques of evaluating prospective alternative uses of funds have been thoroughly described and analyzed in published articles and books by Professor Harold Bierman, George Terborgh, and others. I will not attempt to cover this same ground.

Even though the best capital expenditure plan, short and long range, is made, there still remains the all-important question: Where does the money come from? Barring government subsidy, there are only three sources of funds: the money market, existing funds within the company, and customers.

The money market source is available on a continuing basis only when there is the prospect of profit. Without profit, therefore, capital expenditures would be limited at most to existing funds plus prospective capital consumption allowances; the only incentive to spend these, however, would be to minimize losses which would otherwise occur. And, it should not be forgotten that unless these funds from capital consumption allowances have the purchasing power equivalent to the capital that has been consumed, there is, in effect, capital erosion.

As to the third source—customers—there are also limitations. Although a producer is free to seek for his goods and services whatever prices he thinks are attainable, and although a buyer is free to try to acquire such goods at whatever prices he can, the market always has the final word.

I know that all of you are familiar with the problems of acquiring capital, of evaluating its most advantageous form, and determining the timing and general terms of the financing, so I will forego any discussion of these matters. There is, however, another matter about which frequent misunderstanding seems to exist. In recent years, "cash flow" has become an intriguing term to many. Some imply that it is a more sophisticated measure of profitability rather than simply being only one of the tools utilized in judging investment advisability. But cash flow is not profit! It consists of two entirely different parts—the return *of* investment, or capital consumption allowances, and the return *on* investment, or profit. That part represented by capital consumption allowances is rapidly spent for the new or modernized facilities continually needed for replacement as facilities wear out or become obsolete. The part represented by profit, which is the only part available for dividends to stockholders and for additional investment in the business, provides funds for further modernization and expansion.

The Influence of Taxation on the Investment Climate

My third and final area concerns the importance of a climate for investment.

Although the part that government can constructively play in promoting investment is limited, the part it can play in preventing or curtailing investment is virtually unlimited. For example, government taxation can restrict the incentive and ability to save and productively invest that are essential to economic growth.

I believe that the present-day taxation of corporate income is inequitable and adverse to investment and to economic growth. The major flows of savings into growth-promoting investment and jobs are affected through corporations, yet their incomes, about 8 percent of the national income, are heavily taxed and the part paid out to their owners is taxed again. Many corporations earn no income and hence pay no income tax, although they enjoy the same protection of government accorded those who do pay such taxes. Heavy taxation has thus been concentrated on the more efficient corporations, on the very ones whose ability, investment, and enterprise are most important for economic growth.

I am, of course, mindful of the reductions in federal income tax rates which have occurred in recent years; however, I regard these as the lightening of a deterrent—not as the providing of incentives or the granting of favors. Taxes, by their very nature, are disincentives, and the greater the tax the greater the disincentive.

The present high levels of taxation follow from the high and continually expanding expenditures at all levels of government. It thus follows that ever-increasing taxation can only be effectively interrupted by finding some way to halt or at least slow down the rate of expansion in government expenditures. Admittedly, this is not easy to do.

The problem appears to be one of priorities—how much butter can we afford in a guns and butter budget? One stumbling block to a solution appears to be that, once a given type of government expenditure is initiated, its perpetuation or enlargement becomes a vested right. It is not solely a question as to the merits of various government activities and of their being continued, expanded, or curtailed. It is also a question of whether some or all of them, which should be continued, might not be better carried forward under the auspices of our enterprise system than through an increase in government spending.

Taxes at the state and local levels are also important elements in the investment climate. Perhaps the most dramatic example of this is the case of iron ore mining investments in Minnesota. Because of the tax inequality for the mining industry, new investments were not being made—even though there were substantial reserves of ores. With the passage in 1964 of a constitutional amendment assuring tax equality with other manufacturers for a period of 25 years, investments in taconite processing plants were announced by a number of companies. Northeastern Minnesota has staged a rapid economic comeback and is now enjoying prosperous times. This action—the assurance of tax equality—fostered a favorable climate for investment.

There is another area of taxation—depreciation—which plays a critical role in investment decisions. Financing of replacement should be covered by adequate depreciation allowances. There is a need for realistic, stable, and permanent depreciation allowances, including the investment credit, geared both to the acceleration of obsolescence and to the inflationary erosion of the dollar. In this way, the original purchasing power of capital consumed in production may be recovered, and profits may be more realistically stated. Inadequate depreciation allowances restrict economic growth.

Part of the depreciation problem was alleviated by the accelerated depreciation methods provided in 1954 and by the depreciation reforms involved in both the guideline depreciation procedures and the investment credit in 1962. In the autumn of 1966, I opposed the suspension of the credit, primarily because of the crucial role of investment in fostering economic growth and in holding down inflation, because of the inadequacy of the suspension as a short-term economic measure, and because of the inequity inherent in such a suspension. Its restoration is of utmost importance.

It is my judgment that the best interests of the nation will be served by having depreciation policies which are both competitive with those abroad and which are also a stable and certain part of the tax law—not subject to alteration to meet short-term economic objectives.

Other Factors and the Investment Climate

Another action of government which can aid in promoting a favorable climate for investment is the providing of a dependable medium of exchange. Past and prospective purchasing power erosion complicates and warps business saving, investing, wage, and tax decisions.

Although I have no solution, this much is clear: It has been repeatedly demonstrated that the primary ingredient of price stability is public and legislative determination to have it.

Time does not permit me to discuss many other important elements in the investment climate such as the stability of laws and regulations; reasonable certainty as to government policy on matters which affect investment; government competition with private enterprise; and the freedom of action allowed to management in handling those matters which are properly the subject of private decision.

When factors in the investment climate tend to dampen profits or the prospects of profit, they lessen the incentive to invest. When they tend to strengthen incentive and reduce risk, they speed investment growth.

TAX POLICY AND BUSINESS INVESTMENT

DAN THROOP SMITH

T HE FIRST thing to be said about tax policy and business investment is that tax policy itself ordinarily is not the controlling or even a dominant determinant of business investment. I venture to say this in spite of opinions to the contrary held by some businessmen and by some of my fellow economists.

My purpose in this paper is to describe the many ways in which tax policy might influence business investment. Some of them are familiar, such as the effect of an investment credit on the rate of return. But though the arithmetic has been made familiar, most notably by George Terborgh's thorough analyses, there is still uncertainty as to the significance of marginal changes in rate of return on the amount of investment and, indeed, even on the extent to which decisions may be based on before-tax rather than after-tax returns.

Other ways in which tax policy may influence investments are less familiar and much more subtle. The need for liquidity to meet estate tax burdens in family businesses is presumed to be relevant to the interim commitment of company funds in fixed assets; at least the provisions in the law authorizing tax-free redemptions of stock to pay estate taxes and a ten-year period for payment of these taxes were intended to

encourage continuing vitality as well as the continued independent existence of closely controlled businesses. Even more
elusive is the effect of tax policy on the spirit of entrepreneurship—a spirit which is almost all-important and likely to have
more influence on business investment than rates of return,
costs of capital, and the spreads between the two.

None of the following comments will undertake to add refinements to the very effective detailed analytical work already
done on specific provisions of the law by others, many of whom
have been brought together here as discussants. Rather, my
purpose will be to attempt to present these analyses in perspective. In the process, some of my own skepticism about
the significance of precise pecuniary calculations and differences will become apparent.

Fundamentally, I want to emphasize the overriding importance of the investment climate in influencing the extent of
investment. Recognition of this has become appreciated in
appraising the factors which influence international business
investment. It is generally accepted that no form of tax inducement can draw funds to an otherwise unattractive country.
As one corporate chairman put it, "If the general investment
climate is good, we can assume that the tax system, whatever
its particular structure or rates, will be acceptable; but no
amount of special tax advantages can overcome the fears of a
generally bad situation." Tax laws are a part of the climate,
but unless they are peculiarly bad they are not likely to be a
dominant part.

For the discussion here, I suggest that the domestic investment climate is also, within limitations, a major determinant
of business investment and that the climate consists not only
of the economic situations and forecasts and tax provisions
which can be reduced to pecuniary calculations, but also of a
complex mixture of tradition, law, and actual and presumed
attitudes in government, industry and the general public. However, my assignment is to discuss tax policy and business investment. After these preliminary comments which have been
made to prevent any inference that the subject is all-important,
we can turn to it with the confident expectation that it is both
significant and intellectually interesting.

The range of possible tax influences on business investment

is very broad. In its most comprehensive sense, tax policy must include the policy decision on the aggregate amount of taxation which, in conjunction with expenditure policy, determines the net surplus or deficit. Though the discussion in this paper is presumably intended to stop short of budget policy and be confined to the structure of the tax system, perhaps it is permissible to note that attempts to push total output to the highest possible level through increases in aggregate demand by deficit spending are likely to do more harm than good when they add to the inflationary pressures from excessive wage increases. Recent experience seems to confirm the conclusions of those of us who suspect that we shall have more than sufficient deficits in the ordinary course of events to give whatever expansionary influences may be acceptable without recourse to artificial and perhaps irreversible injections of additional deficit spending. And let it be noted also that a steady erosion of the value of a currency is not necessarily conducive to either maximum or reasonable investment programs.

Specific provisions of the tax law influence business investment by modifying the return on capital investments, the cost of capital funds, and the availability of funds. The tax law will influence investment indirectly through its treatment of outlays for research and innovation, capital gains, new business enterprises, and, as already noted, estate-tax burdens. Within the limits of this paper, it will not be possible to do more than indicate the nature of the relationships and a few of the possible alternative tax rules.

Accelerated Depreciation

Rapid depreciation for tax purposes and an investment credit are the obvious ways to increase the rate of return on investment. The introduction of declining-balance depreciation at double the rate authorized for straight-line depreciation in 1954 and the authorization for shorter lives in the guidelines of 1962, along with the investment credit in the same year, have been the principal relevant additions to the tax law, other than the provisions for five-year amortization of defense facilities during World War II and the Korean emergency.

Faster depreciation may encourage investment in any of

several ways. The most obvious effect, whether faster depreciation arises through the use of the declining-balance method or shorter lives, is a reduction in taxes during the early years of use of a particular item of capital equipment. On a present value calculation, the after-tax return is thereby increased and investment is encouraged. Secondly, the internal flow of available funds is larger and this itself may increase investment. Also, to the extent that funds arising from depreciation are in some way considered more available for capital investment than other funds, the shift in the composition of internal funds through faster tax depreciation gives a further stimulus to investment.

These are familiar and supposedly obvious conclusions, but they are based on the economists' usual assumption that all other things remain unchanged. A more thorough analysis is much more complicated and the results less certain. If, for example, the faster depreciation taken for tax purposes is also used for book purposes, with no change in prices or other costs, net income and the rate of return on specific investments will be reduced, though the cash flow from depreciation will be further increased. The net effects on investment of a reduction in income and an increase in cash flow are by no means certain. It must be noted also that a reduction in net income may discourage outside financing for investment.

And if, to complicate the analysis still further, the faster depreciation is taken into account in fixing production costs for specific products and if pricing is based on costs, the effects become still more uncertain, with a distinction to be made between a partial and full equilibrium analysis. With higher prices, net income and the rate of return may be largely restored, with continued augmented cash flows. When one attempts to carry on to the implications of higher prices on the distribution of income and the shifts in the composition of aggregate demand, the ramifications become too numerous even to list.

A further inducement from faster depreciation must be noted, though reference to it is usually regarded as an insult to those making investment decisions. Nonetheless, I am satisfied that it is still true that in some situations the fact that a piece of equipment has been fully depreciated, or largely depreciated under the declining-balance method, makes it more likely to be considered for replacement. In spite of general recognition that replacements should be made on the basis of a comparison of the direct costs of continued use of old equipment with the total costs of new equipment, or the use of discounted cash flow analyses which ignore depreciation on old equipment, the rule-of-thumb of replacement after full depreciation persists even at lower levels in some major companies. To the extent that it is followed, faster tax depreciation, if adopted for book purposes, will encourage investment.

As one looks ahead, the advantages of shorter lives authorized by the new guidelines will be significantly nullified by the associated reserve ratio test when it becomes fully effective after one life cycle of depreciation. Under this limitation, if actual retirements do not occur within the period assumed for tax depreciation, with a margin of tolerance, subsequent depreciation allowances will be commensurately reduced. No other major industrial country imposes a similar restriction on depreciation deductions. Ingenious though it is, the reserve ratio test will have over a period of time the same depressing effect which was imminent in 1965 when the original three-year grace period expired. The Treasury's action at the time apparently was taken in recognition of the repressive influence of the test, but it merely postponed the ultimate impact.

Some argue that the imminence of a reduction in the tax allowance for depreciation as the ceiling imposed by the reserve ratio test becomes effective will itself encourage new investment, but this conclusion seems to me highly improbable. Hopefully, the reserve ratio test will be removed in the next few years. It is unfortunate that there was not a concerted drive to have its removal coupled with the suspension of the investment credit last year.

The Investment Credit

The investment credit is in many ways analogous to faster depreciation, though it gives a permanent saving in taxes rather than a shift forward in time. Whether one conceives of the investment credit as reducing the cost of an investment, or as increasing the net rate of return from it by lowering the tax on the income derived from it, and whether one regards the reduction in tax as a one-time reduction in the year of acquisition or as amortized over the life of the property, in one way or another there is an increase in both the return on investment and in the cash flow. In comparison to faster depreciation, the advantage is absolute and not merely one in timing. Nor is there any basis for increasing book depreciation or making other adjustments which would reduce book income. And the only possible pressure on prices of products would be towards reduction. For all of these reasons, the investment credit seems preferable to faster depreciation, but this conclusion does not necessarily follow.

The implications of extensive debate among accountants on the book treatment of the investment credit have not received the attention they deserve from economists. It seems unlikely that the full ramifications were considered by those who first proposed the investment credit. The intent was probably simply to give a lower immediate tax. The insistence of accountants on a reserve for future taxes, or for a presumed direct reduction in the cost of equipment with an inaccurate statement of total taxes paid over the entire life of the property, may influence management decisions on investment in ways which have not yet been appreciated.

The continuing controversy on the significance of the investment credit in the utility industries is an extreme example of the way in which a provision of the tax law intended for one purpose may be used to secure a quite different result. The investment credit was adopted to encourage investment. It is debatable whether it should have been given to the utility industries, other than railroads, which had expanding markets and adequate sources of funds. But it was given by the Congress, supposedly to encourage expansion. To the extent that the regulatory agencies reduce the invested capital base or take account of increases in net income of the companies involved for rate purposes, the result is a reduction in utility rates rather than a direct inducement to increase capacity. The intent of Congress thus seems to have been thwarted by some of the regulatory agencies. Further analysis may suggest that some of the treatments required by accountants for financial statements will, if adopted for internal cost and other management accounting, also distort the intended results of the Congress.

If, for example, the investment credit is taken as a reduction in the cost of equipment for book purposes and prices are correspondingly reduced, there will be neither an increase in rate of return nor in internal cash flows.

Credits Versus Rapid Depreciation

Throughout the consideration of the effects of faster depreciation and an investment credit, one must always keep in mind his assumption or belief about the incidence of the corporation income tax. In this country, there seems to be a fairly widespread belief that the corporation income tax to a considerable extent is shifted forward in higher prices. This would seem to imply that a reduction in income taxes would be reflected in lower prices, though the process is not necessarily reversible. But even if not reversible, a reduction in corporate income taxes in the sort of generally inflationary situation to which we appear doomed may keep prices from rising as much as they would otherwise.

To the extent that the tax is shifted and faster depreciation or the investment credit is accordingly reflected in lower prices of products, the intended advantages of higher rates of return on investments and larger total cash flows would seem to be nullified. This is indeed a startling observation and one which has, I believe, not been widely noted in the general enthusiasm for faster depreciation. Virtually all the analysis in the literature thus far has been on the assumption, usually implicit, that the entire benefit of faster depreciation or an investment credit goes to the taxpayer. If this is not valid, we need to think again about our conclusions concerning tax policy.

In the process, however, we must distinguish between the statutory and effective rates of taxation and note the various reasons for the difference. Faster depreciation and an investment credit, though they reduce taxes actually paid, do not change the statutory rate. It may well be that it is the statutory rate which is taken into account in determining price policies and the cut-off points on investments. If this true, a tax reduction through faster depreciation or investment credits may be more effective, as well as more concentrated in its impact, in encouraging investment than a general reduction in the corporation income tax rate. I, for one, suspect that they are, even if corporate taxes are generally shifted forward in prices.

The form of presentation of financial statement specified by the Accounting Principles Board in December, 1966 (Opinion 9) includes income tax under the general heading "cost and expense," along with costs of goods sold and other familiar expense categories. This suggests that the accounting profession has come to think of the income tax as another cost rather than a sharing of profits with government. It is interesting to reflect on the effect of this presentation on management attitudes and on the beliefs of future generations of students concerning the incidence of the tax. Almost as a footnote, one may also observe that the stated "income tax" to be shown in future financial statements is not necessarily the actual amount of tax because "extraordinary items" are to be shown separately at the bottom of the income statement net of specified amounts of "applicable income tax." The total tax thus is known only if one takes the algebraic sum of the two.

A final point may be made on the relative advantages of faster depreciation and investment credits. George Terborgh and others have convincingly demonstrated that the investment credit has a greater pecuniary impact on rate of return than faster depreciation with an equivalent revenue loss. To many, this is conclusive evidence of the advantage of an investment credit. With all respect, one may still argue that the conclusion does not follow because of the different ways in which the two provisions influence the general investment climate.

Recent Tax Policies

The original objection to the proposed investment credit by most members of the business community reflected a concern about what they regarded as a handout from the government and the introduction of another form of intervention in the normal conduct of business affairs. By contrast, faster depreciation, conforming as it would to established practices and desires, would have been welcomed as evidence of understanding of business attitudes.

Nonetheless, it was appreciated by the business community that the investment credit proposal recognized the importance of business investment and the fact that something more than expanded aggregate demand was needed to encourage capital investment. This recognition itself came as a pleasant surprise in 1961 when there was reason to fear that all emphasis might be placed on increasing consumer demand. Thus, the investment climate was improved by the mere proposal of tax relief in this area. A proposal for relief along more traditional lines, that is, through faster depreciation without a reserve ratio test, in my opinion would have been still more effective in improving the climate, even though it gave less pecuniary advantage.

Objections to the removal of the investment credit in 1966 in no way proved that it was the ideal proposal in 1961, as has often been asserted in recent months. Of course, there was objection to any form of tax increase, and the objections to this form of increase were especially emphatic because it seemed to involve a breaking of faith, in view of prior statements that the investment credit should be a permanent feature of the tax law.

The current situation will provide a test of the efficacy of attempts to influence investment in the short run by "on and off" use of the investment credit. My own belief is that it will not be especially significant except for relatively short-lived assets such as trucks, where it may be entirely too effective. There may, to be sure, be some postponement in letting contracts for major expansion when it is known in advance when the credit will again be applicable, again with an accentuation of very short-term fluctuations in activity. But the expected rate of return of major investment programs is usually sufficiently high, or else the investments are made for defensive purposes, to make a modest cost difference not determinative, and once started major programs cannot be discontinued nor will they be long postponed. It seems quite possible that the introduction of a new element of uncertainty, by attempts to use the investment credit for short-term effects, will so weaken the long-run investment climate that the net advantage of the credit will be negligible. This is especially likely to be true if it is thought that the withdrawal of the credit represents bad faith.

On an international comparison, our tax laws are reasonably good in terms of depreciation allowances, with the exception of the reserve ratio test which is not imposed elsewhere. Even after its removal, our estimated service lives will still be somewhat longer than those adopted in other countries, though the guidelines of 1962 were a major reform.

Quite apart from the depreciation allowances and investment credits, one must consider the influence of the corporation income tax on business investment. Its uncertain effects have already been alluded to, with much of the uncertainty arising from the unknown incidence of the tax. But the remarkable thing about the corporation income tax is that regardless of its incidence it is coming to be recognized as a bad tax for a country which aspires to either efficiency or economic growth. To the extent that the tax is shifted forward and reflected in higher prices, it condones and even encourages inefficiency. Since by definition it falls on companies in proportion to their profits, and since profits in general reflect the efficient use of resources, the higher the tax the larger the price umbrella which is extended by the tax-paying companies over the inefficient marginal producers.

One may for social or political reasons tolerate a good deal of inefficiency for the sake of maintaining autonomy in many independent enterprises. I, for one, would do so if for no other reason than what I regard as the social advantage of having resident owner-managers instead of transient professional managers in charge of local industries. This is a personal preference which I seldom find among European acquaintances in either academic or government circles. But if we want the corporation income tax for this reason, we should be forthright about it, which we seldom are.

To the extent that the corporate income tax is not shifted forward, it impedes investment in two ways. It reduces the after-tax rate of return and also reduces the flow of internal funds. A reduction in internal funds, to the extent that it reduces retained earnings instead of dividends, directly limits available funds for investment. Also, with a consequent reduction in stock prices, new issues of equity capital are more costly, in terms of number of shares required for a given amount of funds, than they otherwise would be; this increase in cost of new, outside equity is accentuated if dividends are lower. These propositions take account of price-earnings ratios in stock prices, with recognition that distributed earnings up to a point seem a bit more significant than retained earnings.

The spread between before-tax and after-tax returns, based on a corporate income tax, is clearly significant if the tax is not shifted. By increasing the before-tax return necessary to secure a required after-tax return, the threshold of acceptable investments is raised. In stating and accepting this proposition, I cannot fail to note that there is some evidence that much business investment, at least abroad, is made on a before-tax basis. This was the evidence presented to and accepted by the Richardson Committee in England in 1964 when they concluded that the profits tax did not discourage corporate investment there. One should note that the subject is being investigated again there; with a new full-fledged corporate income tax, the conclusion may well be different.

Taxing Foreign Subsidiaries

I should also report on the basis of research last year that there was also agreement that before-tax returns were the critical measure in determining investments in foreign subsidiaries by the managements of a number of large French companies. The reason given was simply that tax rates and structures changed so often and so much that one would be led astray by making long-term commitments of funds on what was likely to turn out to be temporary tax advantages or disadvantages. This attitude was comparable to that noted earlier in this paper to the effect that a generally good investment climate would have a tax system which was not too bad, while a generally bad climate could not be significantly improved by the most generous tax laws.

In many U.S. companies, the management seems to want to see the results after all returns from investments in foreign subsidiaries are reduced by the U.S. incremental tax, if any, which would be imposed on repatriation of profits, even if there is no plan for repatriation. In this, they seem to be encouraged by most U.S. accountants. By contrast and, in my opinion, more reasonably, British accountants and managements consider the incremental British tax only on those profits which will be repatriated in the near future. This emphasis on returns after-all-taxes on foreign direct investments by U.S. management suggests that the after-tax figure is regarded here as the dominant one in all investment decision, including domestic corporate investment.

A shifting of the corporate income tax forward in higher prices will presumably increase the before-tax rate of return to maintain a desired after-tax rate. The spread may thus seem to be unimportant, to the extent that the tax is in fact shifted. This conclusion, however, though logical, seems too pat. Even if the before-tax rate simply permits the continuation of a needed after-tax rate of return, a very high before-tax cutoff point would appear to have repressive effects. I confess that the point here is elusive, but I cannot dismiss it.

Taxes and the Cost of Funds

The tax system may also directly affect the cost of funds for business investment. The deductibility of interest is notable in decreasing the net cost of borrowing, though one must be careful to recognize that it is the after-tax return from an investment which must exceed the after-tax cost of interest if there is to be an increase in net income. Expanded investments for a before-tax return in excess of the net after-tax cost of borrowed funds can wipe out the net income for common stockholders.

The tax penalty on preferred stock financing is notable. At a 50 percent tax rate, the before-tax return must be double the dividend rate to justify a preferred stock issue. It is regrettable that it was not possible to make preferred dividends deductible in 1954 when the credit for dividends received was adopted. It was considered in the Treasury, but the problems of presentation and the possibilities of windfall gains in a few companies precluded making the proposal to the Congress. The nondeductibility of preferred stock dividends is partially offset by their nontaxability to corporate recipients. If the amount of preferred stock which might be issued did not exceed the demand from corporate investors, the interplay of these two provisions might wash out. But this is not the case, and the yield must be sufficient to attract noncorporate investors, just as the yield of tax-exempt municipal bonds must be high enough to appeal to marginal buyers who are far below the highest tax brackets. The tax advantages to the higher bracket investors in both cases are not reflected in lower financing costs to those seeking funds.

Double Taxation

This is not the time to recapitulate the familiar arguments about the double taxation of dividend income, tracing through the analysis on the alternative assumptions of shifting and non-shifting of the corporate income tax. But it should be pointed out that, with the exception of Great Britain, all changes in other countries in the past decade have been in the direction of partial relief. Germany has a lower rate of tax on distributed income, and this treatment was recommended for the Common Market by the Neumark Committee. France last year adopted a credit for stockholders of part of the corporate tax, a system also used in Belgium. Japan has both a lower rate on distributed earnings and a credit to stockholders. And the Carter Commission in Canada has recommended a full allowance of the corporate tax against the individual income tax on dividends after gross-up.

On an international comparison, our statutory rate of corporate tax and our full double taxation of dividend income place our tax system at a pronounced disadvantage from the standpoint of tax burdens through equity financing.

In all candor, however, one must recognize that investment in manufacturing industries is seldom pushed to the margin described in economics textbooks where returns just exceed the cost of funds. The spread is usually sufficiently great, or the need for the investment so pressing on defensive grounds, as to permit appreciable decreases in returns and increases in costs of funds from bad tax policies without throttling investment. This is not to say that investment would not be greater if more internal funds were available or if the before-tax cut-off point were not lower, but the consequences of taxation are not to be found primarily through its impact at the no-profit point where marginal returns equal marginal costs. In the housing industry, investment may be pushed closer to the margin, though it appears that even then it is the availability rather than the cost of funds which is critical. In those utilities with expanding markets, rate policy seems more important than tax policy.

Taxes, Savings, and Investment

The distortions and repressions regarding business investment because of the corporation income tax are, of course, directly related to its rate, though the relation is probably not linear. A modest rate can be sustained with minimum disturbance, but at very high rates the influences can be overwhelming, as we know from these brief periods when excess profits taxes have continued beyond war periods. A value-added tax as a partial substitute for the corporation income tax seems preferable in virtually all respects. It can be especially effective in encouraging investment, if the tax paid on the purchase of capital equipment is allowed as an immediate offset against the tax due on sales. But I have urged the advantages of a value-added tax over a corporation income tax so many times in recent years that I shall not presume to do so again on this occasion.

The effects of tax policy on the aggregate supply of capital involve considerations of the marginal propensity to save at different income levels, and on this subject we cannot be sure of the effects of taxation. Recent research and theory emphasize a distinction between regular and expected income, and the different attitudes when at any given level of income one is confronted with a reduction in his standard of living in contrast to a potential improvement. Suffice it to say that our high bracket individual rates are by no means conducive to savings.

Several proposed changes in the tax law would be significantly adverse to savings and the continuation of existing capital, perhaps seriously so. A presumptive realization of capital gains at death or on gift would absorb a segment of existing capital. Any increases in death duties would also absorb individually-owned capital. An increase in the capital gains taxes on reinvested gains would be particularly onerous. In all of these cases, there is not any intention to imply that existing physical assets would be dismantled or consumed. Rather, new savings by others, potentially available for new investment, would be used to buy existing assets.

An increase in the capital gains tax would also discourage the entrepreneurs who form new ventures, as well as the investors in them. If one believes that a good deal of our economic vitality comes from the innovations introduced by new companies, a curtailment of entrepreneurship and investment outlets of this sort would be undesirable. From the standpoint of capital gains taxation, our laws are already about the worst in the world from the standpoint of the effect on business investment, with the exception of the new British provisions adopted last year. If Canada adopts the recent proposals of the Royal Commission there, it will outdo the United Kingdom in this respect.

However, apart from the existence of our capital gains tax, our laws are probably the best in the world in giving special treatment to new and closely-controlled businesses. The provisions regarding stock redemption to pay estate taxes and the right to spread estate tax payments over ten years have already been noted. In addition, one should note the provision for ordinary instead of capital loss deductions for investors in the stock of small corporations (section 1244), the right of closely-controlled corporations to elect to be taxed as partnerships (subchapter S), the lower rate of corporate tax on the first $25,000 of taxable income, and the first-year 20 percent deduction on the first $10,000 of investment in certain depreciable property (section 179).

Even rather detailed technical points may have considerable significance. For example, the regulations were changed following the adoption of the Internal Revenue Code of 1954 to permit investment in any active trade or business to relieve a company from the penalty tax on unreasonable accumulation of surplus. Previously, a strict rule was applied and investment had to be made in the existing trade or business, a limitation which was stultifying for a management which chose to diversify or change its activity. In other countries, small ventures are usually thought of as inefficient and not likely to be a source of significant innovation. Comparable relief provisions are seldom found abroad, though economic vitality might be increased if some of our precedents were followed.

Taxes and Innovation

Our tax treatment of research and development expenditures are also relatively favorable. The option to capitalize or deduct them currently permits new companies to postpone deductions until they are profitable, while others may get the full advantage of immediate deductions. We have not gone so far as Canada formerly did in giving a deduction in excess of outlay, nor do we extend the option to the equipment used in research. The former seems unnecessary, but the latter should be done now that the law would recover as ordinary income any profit up to original purchase price of depreciable property which was sold after being written off as a current expense.

But innovation in industry, large and small, seems to depend more on the general attitude of management than on any specific provision of the tax law regarding research. Europeans often complain of their inability to compete effectively because of our very large research outlays, but many of those familiar with attitudes and policies on both sides of the Atlantic insist that a willingness to build capacity ahead of demand and a vigorous competition in which the laggard falls by the wayside is at least as important as research expenditures. This *élan vital* which we still have depends on many things other than the tax law, though certain proposed changes in the law which are deemed desirable by some according to their concepts of equity could be repressive. Our economy thus far seems to have enough vitality to survive in spite of the attempts of those who seem more concerned to redivide the gross national product pie than to increase its size. The adoption of similar policies in the developing countries where entrepreneurship has not yet developed may be more serious.

Lest the foregoing statement be taken to mean that we can be indifferent to the effects of tax policy on business investment in this country, let me say that this is by no means the case. Faster depreciation, lower corporate tax rates, special provisions for small business and research activities, and a reasonable recognition of the differences between income and capital are all important to continued growth here. The uncertainties which I have noted concerning the precise impact of certain provisions of the law do not mean that we can ignore tax considerations generally. I do indeed fear a deterioration in our investment and entrepreneurial climate in this country through developments, including the tax laws. But much of the adverse impact of the so-called "reforms" designed to redistribute income and wealth will come, I believe, at least as much through their effects on climate as through their pecuniary results.

Taxes and Types of Investment

Comments on the effects of tax policy on one particular form of business investment are, unfortunately, so timely that they are offered here even though they were certainly not expected by those who arranged this program. Direct business investment abroad was wisely excluded from the so-called interest equalization tax when it was adopted in 1964. Evidence submitted to the Congress in 1961 and 1962 had, one hoped, demonstrated both the importance of income from direct investment abroad for our balance of payments and the need for continuing investment to maintain the flow of income from many existing investments. Recent proposals from various sources suggest that this has not yet been recognized and that a penalty tax may be proposed on additional direct investment.

Even for those of us who agree that as a nation we are financially overcommitted abroad, it seems unwise and, indeed, foolhardy to take action which would jeopardize the value of our principal foreign assets. If sufficiently high, a penalty tax could deter even those investments which are necessary to maintain the flow of income from existing activities. Proposed regulations under section 482, if adopted, will themselves harass and penalize foreign direct investment.

Economists now argue as to whether direct investment should be viewed on an "organic" or "incremental" basis. The latter concept suggests that each increment of investment produces its own increment of income with, by implication, the income from previous investments continuing independently. For those of us who have had responsibility to decide the timing as well as the fact of major investments, it is, I believe, clear that when a new product or process is available, undue postponement may not only represent an opportunity forever lost, but impair the value and income from an established business. But since this fact of business life has not been and perhaps cannot be demonstrated statistically, at least until after the damage has been done, it has not been accepted by many of those who may determine future tax policy. New entrants and completely new ventures in foreign activities by established companies may be treated on an incremental basis, though even for them postponement may make later entry impossible or prohibitively expensive.

Since foreign direct investment appears to be the form of business investment most likely to be subject to selective influence by a change in tax policy in the near future, I shall conclude my paper with the foregoing rather categorical remarks on the subject. They are intended to be provocatively emphatic and to show my real concern that our tax policy may go woefully astray in this respect.

DISCUSSION AND COMMENTS ON PAPERS BY MR. TYSON AND PROFESSOR SMITH

Professor William J. Baumol

This is a session on which it is really terribly difficult to comment because the other speakers have tried extremely hard to be right in what they say and this puts the discussant at a great disadvantage. As a result, I am going to try to do something harder. I am going to try to say things that are probably very wrong.

I am going to spend very little time commenting on specific points in the papers. In fact, I may say almost nothing about them at all. I gather some of the other discussants will be more directly relevant. I am going to talk, in effect, about something else; that is, I am going to talk in the few minutes that we are allowed about some of the social implications of what has been said. If I judge correctly the temper of the group and of the audience, I think I am going to say some things which you will like and some things which you will very much dislike, though I hope I will stir up a little interest.

But, first, let me just make a minor point about Professor Smith's paper. He stressed the fact that the investment credit or accelerated depreciation may not have some of the consequences which seem obviously to follow from them. Specifically, he notes that they may be shifted forward so that,

37

instead of leading to increased profits, they may instead result
in lower prices. This, of course, is very true and it was very
helpful of him to bring it out. I wish merely to comment
that a reduction in prices too may be a very desirable consequence of both of these measures; that is, it may be expansionary either to stimulate the production of capital by making
investment more profitable or to stimulate demand by making
final products less expensive. In sum, the fact that these
benefits are shifted forward is of some analytic interest but,
from the point of view of the policymaker, either of the possible consequences may enable him to achieve his ultimate
objective.

But the two main subjects which I would like to discuss
are the effects of the corporate income tax, and, second, some
of the consequences of corporate investment for the social
climate and the level of taxation, both of which have been
cited as essential determinants of the level of investment
itself. I am going to argue that business investment, though
it has all of the obvious consequences that have been claimed
for it, has in addition some indirect consequences which are
not generally recognized and which themselves tend to cause
some changes in the business climate, social circumstances,
and the tax structure, and that they in turn affect the level
of investment.

But first the corporate income tax. The point has been
made that the corporate income tax, as is well recognized,
distorts some of the decision processes within the corporation.
For example, it has been pointed out that it makes it far less
profitable to employ preferred stock as a method of financing.

As a matter of fact a group of us has recently been involved
in some research which shows that the potential distorting
influences of the corporation income tax on the methods of
business financing are far greater than might have been sus-
pected. That is, under the peculiar distortion introduced by the
corporate income tax, it almost pays corporations, from the
point of view of those who invest funds in them, to play a
sort of Russian roulette with their funds. It pays corporations
to engage in a degree of leverage, a degree of debt financing
far greater than might have been rational in its absence, and
the reason is very simple.

If a corporation obtains its funds through debt rather than through equity, it acquires them by a method which enables those who provide the funds to escape the effects of the corporation income tax and thereby makes it possible to provide those funds more cheaply. It has recently been pointed out by economic theory that it pays the investor to have the corporation to do this because, while increased leverage is risky from the point of view of the corporation—it increases the amount of the fixed obligations which the corporation undertakes—in fact, the private investor has available to him the protection of a sort of homemade insurance policy. For example, if the corporation doubles the amount of leverage (the proportion of debt in its capital) and thereby reduces the amount of tax payment which it incurs, the investor can compensate for any resulting reduction in the safety of his own equity holdings by shifting a part of his funds from equity to debt, increasing the proportion of bonds in his personal portfolio. He can, in fact, decrease his risk in precisely the proportion that the corporation increases its risk and thereby end up in precisely the risk position he would have otherwise been in, and yet in the process legally evade the tax obligation. This may be a good thing for the individual investor, who reacts to the corporation income tax, but it surely represents a serious distortion in the corporation's own financial structure.

But I was really interested more in discussing the effect of these taxes on society rather than on the corporation itself, and I want to point out that one of the generally unnoticed and serious consequences of the corporation income tax is the way in which it distorts the allocation of resources of the economy and how, in particular, it causes a serious misallocation of resources to the public sector. To see how this problem arises, we must examine from the economist's point of view the basic principle for the optimal allocation of resources to the public sector. Consider a proposal for the building of a new road, or the construction of a new dam. When should such a project be undertaken? The answer is that it is desirable, provided that the rate of yield of the resources which are taken out of the private sector is at least as great as what those resources would have returned in the private sector. That is to say, if those resources could have returned to the economy 10 percent in the private sector and only bring in 5 percent in the public sector, then the transfer of those resources clearly represents a 5 percent loss in output to society.

What has the corporation income tax to do with this? The answer is that it has given two sets of inconsistent signals to the conscientious planner who wants to use the opportunity cost criterion which I have just proposed. Why? Because resources which are used in the construction of dams or other public projects are taken from two sectors of the economy, to simplify the matter. They are taken either from consumers or from private business. Whenever cement is used in the construction of a dam, either some private industry or some consumer is deprived of that raw material. Let us see what happens when this cement is taken away from a consumer or a firm.

If it is taken away from a private consumer who does not pay a corporate income tax on his own uses of these goods, he is, in effect, earning a different rate of return on resources than does the corporate sector. What do I mean by that? Well, in the corporate sector, if the market requires that stockholders earn an 8 percent rate of return, then it means that *before taxes* this corporation must be producing a yield something of the order of magnitude of 16 percent. That is to say, each bag of cement taken away from this type of investment deprives society of an output which yields 16 percent.

On the other hand, the private individual who is buying government bonds at a rate of return, say, of 5 percent, obtains a marginal yield much lower than 16 percent. Since a government project cannot simultaneously provide a return of 8 and 16 percent, the resources which are taken out of the private sector and put into public investment must violate either the one signal or the other. For example, if the government undertakes a project offering benefits equivalent to a 6 percent return on its investment any resources obtained from the business sector must represent a waste since in business investment they can yield 16 percent.

Thus either the resources taken from consumers or those taken from business must represent an inefficient use and hence a misallocation of resources, and this as a result of the corporation income tax.

Now let me turn to my second general subject, the social consequences of business investments. Here I would like to raise some delicate issues. You know, in some respects business investment is like motherhood. You well remember that the desirability of motherhood was unquestioned for a very long time—until psychiatrists began to examine the institution.

It will also be recognized that the upshot of this investigation was that a mother is really a pretty good thing to have, but it was a good thing also that the subject was examined. I think we are going to end up much the same way when I discuss the role of business investment.

I am going to argue that some of the social climate and some of the taxes that are plaguing society and industry today are an inescapable, though unintentional, consequence of the very success of business investment, of the very progress that it occasions. Let me be specific about what I mean.

We have noticed in recent years that in urban communities the costs of government operations, the costs of provision of their services have gone up at a tremendous rate. Public school systems are threatened constantly with deterioration and their costs go up far, far faster than costs in the economy generally. Costs per student go up far more quickly than the costs of automobiles or telephones or electric service.

The reason for the difference when one thinks about it is really quite obvious. Let's consider the difference between the technology of education and the technology of the production of the manufactured good. In the manufactured good there is all sorts of opportunity for increases in productivity and business is always extremely ingenious and effective in taking advantage of these opportunities.

In teaching, there is also some room for increases in productivity. Most obviously we can increase productivity by increasing class size so that we have more students per teacher. But when elementary school classes get beyond, say, 50 students, we begin to grow nervous about the effects on quality of education. Other ways of raising productivity in the services are equally likely to cause deterioration in their products.

The result is that while productivity increases in the manufacturing sector, spectacularly and consistently, in education and the other services, in the nature of the case, productivity rises slightly and lags in the long run.

Because of the increase in productivity resulting from the very effectiveness of investment in the business sector, costs in manufacturing rise relatively slowly and wages are enabled to rise to share in the prosperity of industry, a fact of which industry is very proud. But in the services such as education one runs into two alternatives. Either wages will fall further and further behind so that the teacher's earnings trail behind those of a plumber or a janitor, or, somehow, wages will gradually keep pace but then, because there are no offsetting increases in productivity, the costs of these institutions will rise cumulatively year after year, and that rise will be faster, the more effective and the more successful are the efficiencies introduced by the success of business investment.

This means that the rising costs of the supply of urban services are not an accident. They follow from the fact that in the nature of their structure they cannot keep up with the spectacular rate of progress achieved by American industry and so the relative costs of municipal administration must inevitably rise. It is no accident that reform mayors and reform governors who are elected on a platform promising spectacular savings in costs, are time after time forced to propose budgets that are unique in the history of their areas.

I, therefore, argue not that there is anything to be questioned about the desirability of business investment. I am not suggesting that it should be discouraged in any way. I imply, rather, that in addition to its direct consequences, the prosperity which it provides to the economy, the abundance and high standard of living which it makes available, investment, like all good things, has some more subtle and indirect consequences of which we must not lose sight and for which we must be prepared to take responsibility.

Professor Harold Bierman, Jr.

I will start off with a few comments on Professor Smith's paper. I agree more readily with the later Smith who states that "the aspects of tax policy are all-important to continued growth here," than the early Smith who states, "tax policy itself is not the controlling or even a dominant determinant of business investment."

A small percentage of the total investment made in the United States may be undertaken with no analysis or on a before-tax basis but business managers controlling the largest amount of investment funds want to know the after-tax return or net present value an investment would generate.

Saying that taxes are a dominant determinant of business investment does not preclude admitting that there are other important influences. It may be that one can reconcile the difference in point of view by saying that a bad tax policy is more effective in stifling investment than a good tax policy is effective in stimulating investment where the investment climate is otherwise bad.

To stimulate investment, Smith favors accelerated depreciation over the use of an investment credit but confuses the comparison by stating that the advantage of the credit is absolute while the advantage of the faster depreciation is merely one in timing. Both the accelerated depreciation and the investment credit gain their benefits by increasing the value of the investment. They do it in slightly different ways, but one shouldn't speak in terms of "merely" a change in the timing. This is a real benefit and it should be noted as such.

I could spend a great deal of time with Professor Smith's discussion of the economic consequences of accelerated depreciation. His analysis rests on faulty accounting—using tax depreciation accruals for book purposes—combined with faulty economic analysis, namely the basing of prices on the allocation of faulty depreciation charges.

He goes on and discusses the accounting for the investment credit stating there is no basis for increasing book depreciation or making other adjustments that would reduce book income. This is not correct. There is sound basis for increasing some expense. I wouldn't necessarily call it "book depreciation." It is an adjustment to another account. There is justification for reducing book income. That is, if you don't make this adjustment, book income is increased by the purchase of a new investment, and it is not obvious that this should take place.

The statement is made by Professor Smith that it is coming

to be recognized that the corporate income tax is a bad tax from the point of view of efficiency and economic growth. One might say that it is coming to be recognized that all taxes are bad taxes and they all interfere with efficiency and economic growth. It is not obvious, and I don't think it's becoming recognized that the corporate tax is any more harmful than many other taxes, especially if the rates of those other taxes become excessively high.

Before one shifts to something like a value added tax you must consider the fact that when a profitable firm, a firm that has a large net taxable income, now looks at a risky investment opportunity it has a near perfect loss offset. That is, if the loss takes place, it can be deducted from other income. Before going to a value-added tax or to another method of taxation, one has to give serious thought to the consequences of abandoning this very nice aspect of making the government an implicit partner in risky investments.

There is a very bold statement by Smith that distributed earnings up to a point are more significant than retained earnings. I, like Professor Baumol, have been studying the tax effects of investment. It is not obvious that all corporations ought to be paying dividends. Some corporations should not be paying any dividends, let alone a significant percentage of their earnings in dividends. Admittedly, there are conflicting views. Empirical studies have been made by Lintner and Gordon, and a fine theoretical article has been written by Miller and Modigliani. On the one hand, we have statements that corporations should pay X percent of their earnings in dividends. On the other hand, we have statements that it really doesn't make any difference what dividend policy is followed.

I suggest that it makes a lot of difference, but not necessarily in the direction that has been indicated by Professor Smith. Retained earnings may be more significant than dividends.

Reference is made to decision practices in England that ignore future taxes to be paid upon repatriation of income, and making investment analyses on a before-tax basis. I don't doubt that investment decisions are made throughout the world on faulty bases. But I am not sure to what extent that is relevant to us. Certainly we can agree that investment decisions should be on an after-tax basis.

A reference is made to the cost of preferred stock, comparing this with the cost of debt, one being deductible for tax purposes, the other not deductible. We might toss in also the cost of common stock, since dividends on common stock are not deductible for tax purposes. I think there is a major problem here, one that sooner or later one has to face up to. At this point I could make reference to the correct statement by Professor Baumol that there is an incentive for a high degree of leverage. I will extend it one step further and say there is an incentive, if we consider taxes, for 100 percent leverage, for 100 percent debt. This capital structure doesn't necessarily increase the risk. While we could have stockholders turn in their stock for debt, this is not a tax-free transaction. However, new issues of debt could be issued to the stockholders. Now, it's true that the Internal Revenue Service will start objecting when the leverage reaches a certain point but this merely requires that we conform to the institutional constraints.

I stress the fact that as business managers become more sophisticated, the U.S. Treasury is going to have a problem. I see a problem not only in terms of capital structure, but in all aspects of dividend policy and other financial policy decisions.

Professor Smith spoke of death duties and investments. I might say that this sort of partial analysis is dangerous. If one were to eliminate death duties and keep the same revenue requirement, he would be replacing it with other types of taxes. The query would be: What types of taxes and what effect would these have on investments?

Reference was made to stock options and their being important to stimulating the economy and incentives to management. I certainly do not think this is so. Stock options are very nice rewards for managers to receive, and the tax treatment makes them even more attractive. If I were a manager, I would want the special tax treatment to continue in the future, just as I, as an academic, like several gifts that are given me because of the nature of my position.

But to say that stock options are a necessary condition for

having a stimulating and growing economy is not correct. I cannot accept that theory. This point of view shortchanges the competitive spirit of American managers. I don't think that the tax treatment of stock options is an essential part of the incentive system.

I would guess that one of the most unsettling of things to investment decisions is change in the tax laws, especially changes that seem to be undesirable. Even desirable changes are frequently not well understood. For example, the investment credit was not welcomed by the business community with the enthusiasms that it merited. The abandonment of the credit was greeted with groans and forecasts of doom.

If I am correct, then we must be very careful that the revenue code as it affects business must not be changed frequently and the changes must be accompanied by educational campaigns.

It should also be remembered that personal taxes affect business decisions. Professor Baumol spoke of the corporate income taxes affecting business decisions. I am not sure whether business decisions are affected more by corporate taxes or by personal taxes.

Individuals pay personal taxes but equally important they are also persons who make business decisions. Thus, psychologically, they carry over reactions from preparing their personal income tax returns to their operations as business managers.

In closing my comments on Professor Smith's paper I stress the necessity of appreciating the fact that investors, whether individual or corporate, must approach an investment opportunity in terms of a comparison of the amounts that can be expected to be retained for consumption or dividends. This means that investments must be analyzed on an after-tax basis, and the persons preparing our tax code should assume they are dealing with reasonably rational individuals. Any other conclusion would move us from any possibility of arriving at an easily understood, fair, and efficient tax system.

I'll move on to my comments on Mr. Tyson's paper. First I would like to draw your attention to an omission, rather than something that was said by Mr. Tyson. At one place he states that U.S. Steel determines "the expected costs and benefits for each year at the same period, comparing these benefits in some manner with the required capital outlay." He later states that "any resultant numbers expressed in such terms as greater return, pay-back period or net present value are no better than the underlying assumptions on which they are based."

The first statement raises my curiosity, and while I agree completely with the second statement, it increases my curiosity even further.

The manner in which U.S. Steel Corporation, other steel corporations and, indeed, other corporations compare the expected benefits and costs, and the criteria used to accept or reject investments is of great importance to our economy. I think it is of crucial importance.

Here we have private enterprise deciding whether to replace plant and equipment. I am completely ignorant about the criteria used by major American corporations, although I shouldn't say completely. I have seen numerous surveys that indicate certain criteria that are used: for example, two-year paybacks, and 20 percent returns on investment.

I suggest that these criteria can be of crucial importance. There are many references in Mr. Tyson's paper to mutually exclusive investments and more than a hint that internal capital rationing is taking place. I sincerely hope that the techniques being used to make these decisions are based on reasonable underlying assumptions.

For example, reference is made to the cost of financing. What does United States Steel consider to be its time value of money and the time value of money of its investors? The answer to this question will, of course, influence the investment decisions that are being made.

Through the years literature coming from the United States Steel Corporation, talks and reports, have too frequently been focused on the difficulties and hazards facing the steel industry and there have been few references to the opportunities. The capital-erosion-because-of-inflation argument has almost become an obsession with the officers of the firm, and this fear of inflation strongly influenced the willingness of U.S. Steel to innovate.

I cannot guess whether the investors of U.S. Steel are better off or worse off because of the monetary and fiscal policies of the federal government that resulted in the inflation after the Second World War. How did these investors fare as compared with investors in U.S. savings bonds, insurance policies, and pensions?

I suspect that investors in steel companies did reasonably well both absolutely and relatively but this line of argument is not apt to convince the chairman of the board of U.S. Steel. In fact, it is not likely to convince the chairman of the finance committee.

I do agree that it is possible that an investor in a long-lived asset can get hurt financially when inflation is combined with the current tax code relating to depreciation and with prices that cannot be readily increased.

As a partial solution, I am pleased to repeat a suggestion I have made elsewhere, corporations should be allowed to expense equipment for tax purposes upon acquisition. Allowing corporations to do this would remove uncertainty from business decision making with little or no cost to the government.

I might say, in reference to short-lived equipment, that there is little or no benefit to corporations in having the privilege of expensing as they currently have. This is an opportunity for the government to reduce or eliminate a great deal of mystery that currently exists. After looking at the tax code in some detail, I must say that if I were an officer of a corporation, or an accountant for a corporation, I don't think I'd ever retire any equipment. The tax implications would be too complex. There is a great deal of paperwork associated with justifying the retirement. We must decide whether it is a normal retirement or an abnormal retirement and so forth. I really don't understand the tax code on this particular point and this is after a considerable amount of effort.

Mr. Tyson has said that the part the government can constructively play in promoting investment is limited. We all understand what he means by this statement, but I do take exception. If we take as given the present level of investment with the present tax laws, we might be able to modify the tax laws so as to increase the level of investment.

The immediate write-off of equipment would accomplish a promotion of investment. It would certainly eliminate for a large percentage of investment the inflationary erosion of the dollar question that has so bothered the steel industry.

Mr. Tyson's paper emphasizes well the need for a tax code that is easily understood by investors, that is a code that is not apt to be changed adversely for corporate investors in the near future and that supplies incentives for corporations to undertake investments in long-lived assets.

Our present tax code fails the "understanding" test. The off-and-on manipulations of the investment tax credit cause it to fail the "stability" test, and it is clear that some business executives are not pleased with the type of investment incentives supplied by the present code.

It would be incorrect to interpret my remarks to reflect complete dissatisfaction with the present tax code. However, it is clear to anyone who has studied the code that it is excessively complex. Only an expert, and he needs a bit of perseverance and luck, can understand the economic implications to investment decisions. At the risk of adding more complexities, I would like to see the code simplified. One way in which the code could be simplified is to permit immediate write-offs for a wide classification of equipment.

In conclusion, I challenge industry to recheck its criteria for evaluation of investments and I challenge the federal government to improve the climate for making investment decisions.

Professor William T. Hogan

I would like to address myself at the outset to the 7 percent tax investment credit which has received considerable attention here this afternoon. When it became law with the Revenue Act of 1962 it was considered, along with the change in depreciation guidelines, to be depreciation reform. The need for some type of depreciation reform was recognized by virtually everyone at that time and the two measures were designed to accomplish this. The 7 percent tax investment credit was supported by two factions: the first was interested in some change in the tax laws to solve the depreciation problem, while the second looked on it as a stimulant for economic growth.

At the time of its passage, the 7 percent tax credit was not thought of as a tool or means for managing the economy, i.e., something which could be turned off and on to either diminish or stimulate economic activity. It was not until 1966, when capital spending reached an all time high, that there was agitation for the repeal or suspension of the 7 percent credit in order to curtail expenditures for plant and equipment which some considered to be an inflationary force. Capital goods expenditures had increased from $45 billion in 1964 to $52 billion in 1965 and, finally, to a projected $61 billion in 1966. So in September of 1966, the tax credit was suspended with the promise that it would be reinstated in January, 1968. The suspension of the tax credit was to be an experiment which hopefully would diminish the rate of increase of capital expenditures. I would like to emphasize the fact that it was an experiment. The credit had made a contribution to capital investment and its suspension was supposed to work in the opposite direction. The problem of inflation, which was significant at the time, required that some short-run measures be taken for a quick solution. There was considerable debate as to whether the suspension of the tax credit would help in the short run. Without question it would affect capital spending over a period of time, but many felt it would take several months or longer for this effect to take place.

In order to determine whether or not the suspension was effective as a short-run tool to cool off the economy and stem inflation, we at Fordham University undertook a survey which covered 160 of the largest firms in the United States to ascertain what effect, if any, the suspension of the tax credit had on their capital spending in the few months after September, 1966. We also included a fair cross-section of small business to determine the effect of the credit's suspension on the small firm. The data gathered from the large companies presented a rather complete picture of their situation, however, the data on the smaller firms are not as complete.

The results of the survey of the large business firms indicate that the suspension of the tax credit made virtually no difference in the few months after September, 1966. This did not come as a surprise for the bulk of the expenditures made by big corporations involves heavy equipment and this, in turn, requires long-range planning, as well as a long time for installation. In many instances, the expenditures are planned to cover a period of two or three years. Thus, 87 percent of the firms indicated that there was no effect on their spending for the few months after September, 1966, and 74 percent indicated that the suspension of the credit had no effect on their capital expenditure budget for the calendar year 1967. Of the 26 percent who said that the credit had some effect on their 1967 capital expenditure budget, nine firms reported a reduction of 5 percent, 14 firms reported a reduction of 10 percent, while a 20 percent reduction was reported by three of the firms. Only one firm reported that its capital expenditures for 1967 were drastically cut by 50 percent.

Thus, it would seem as far as a short-run means for managing the economy was concerned, the suspension of the tax credit was not particularly effectual. This certainly was true of the large corporations. In a number of cases large firms did not spend their planned capital budget for 1966 simply because deliveries of equipment were not made on schedule, due to the fact that equipment builders had full order books and were a bit slow in meeting their commitments.

In the instances where large firms curtailed spending because of the suspension of the tax credit, a number indicated it was on small items such as office furniture, business machines, small tools, and the like. Here, little if any lead time is required, for the items in question are, so to speak, bought off the shelf of the supplier. The total suspension of expenditures involved for such items would amount to 3 percent or 4 percent of capital investment.

The one noticeable cutback in expenditures among large companies was in the railroad car business. Many orders were cancelled; in fact, the cutback by the beginning of 1967 was quite severe. In contrast to this, one large company had a $400 million plant under construction, but this was not slowed up at all by the suspension of the credit. The schedule had to be pushed ahead so that the various components would fit together and plant production could be coordinated as each unit came on stream.

I believe some comments which were made in connection with answers to the survey questionnaire will confirm the foregoing statements. A paper company official reported: "Our cycle of planning, commitments and expenditures is from 2 to

3 years. Thus we could not react in 1967 to the suspension."

A steel company executive stated "because of the way the suspension was placed and because we had committed ourselves to a major $16½ million expansion program for the year 1967 in early 1966, we were completely covered for this major program. . . . However, we have considered a delay in placing orders during the second half of 1967. We will, however, curtail the placement of orders if there is no repeal of the suspension." He added that "As a supplier to the capital goods industry, we are noticing a reduction in spending in 1967 and we think there will be a delay in the placement of orders until the repeal of the investment credit is clarified."

An automaker reported: "We cannot point to any specific spending changes because the 7 percent investment tax credit was suspended. We view the 7 percent investment tax credit as one of the many economic and financial factors in making investment decisions, and therefore, find it difficult to isolate the specific effect of this one element."

Turning to small business, and here our data were quite sparse, there seemed to be an indication that many firms had curtailed capital expenditures during the months after September, 1966. This is primarily due to the fact that such firms purchase small pieces of equipment in which there is relatively little lead time since the items are bought out of stock. In fact, there appeared to be a direct relationship between the size of the firm and the effect of the suspension of the investment tax credit. Those firms which produced special machine tools felt that the suspension had quite an effect on their sales and found that there was a great deal of shifting and cancelling of orders. Thus, on balance, the suspension of the 7 percent credit did not appear to be an effective, short-run tool for stemming inflation. However, the suspension did cause much uncertainty among businessmen who make long-range plans for capital investment. They had regarded it as a permanent part of the tax law and, in fact, had been assured through 1966 that it would remain a permanent part of the tax law, and those plans were made with it in mind.

Fortunately, equipment which was used for water and air pollution control was not involved in the tax credit suspension. Plans for greater investment in this area have been made throughout industry. In fact, with regulations on air and water pollution getting more stringent every year, there will undoubtedly be billions of dollars spent over the next 15 years to prevent air and water pollution. This expenditure, in almost every instance, does not add to the productive capacity of a company. Products are not made faster, they are not made cheaper. Thus, the cost must be borne over and above costs of production and is a social cost rather than an economic one. It has been suggested that this social cost be borne in part by the community through an additional tax investment credit which would allow companies to deduct up to 15 percent of the cost of such equipment from their taxes. This has been recognized in a number of foreign countries where a company may write off as much as 50 percent of the cost of a water or air pollution control facility in the first year of its operation.

Some mention was made of the foreign tax laws and how we probably are as well off now in terms of depreciation as most of the countries around the world.

I would very much tend to agree with this, however, it is only since 1962 that we brought ourselves into this position. We were woefully short up until that time. And it was because of the change in the guidelines and the 7 percent credit, which I sincerely hope will be reinstated, that we were able to catch up and, in many instances, surpass the foreign competition in a number of industries.

Questions from the Floor

Question: In several of the papers, particularly Mr. Tyson's and Professor Hogan's, the question of how great the capital investment was in relation to the economy and how much effect it had in overheating was hinted at. But there wasn't any very specific measurement.

I would like to ask this. The amount of capital investment as a percentage of the gross national product was hardly increased since the early 1950s. I made a study of that and it runs around 7.5 percent, a little bit above or a little bit below. But with all of the incentives, the investment credit and the guidelines did nothing more than keep the investment as a percentage of gross national product where it was before they went into effect.

While I think that that was very good, that was essential and helpful, the incentives didn't really increase by what I consider to be a rational measure of their impact. They just kept us where we were.

Now, I think it ought to be stressed that the real test of whether we have too much investment, whether the investment is boiling up and inflationary, is the percentage of gross national product, not the absolute amount. I think the absolute amount is almost irrelevant.

That's my first question. I have one other short question for Professor Smith.

That is: What grounds does he have for his hope that the reserve ratio will be eliminated?

Mr. Tyson: I think the questioner is correct that the level of capital expenditures in 1966 did not even get back to the same ratio as had existed in the mid-1950s, '55, '56 and '57, that was the reason that in my paper I made the statement that in my judgment the increase in capital investment that had occurred since the early 1960s was a boon rather than a boom.

Perhaps I did not get the thought across but it was my intention to stress the very point that he made.

Professor Smith: I have no specific basis other than the logic of the desirability of getting rid of the reserve ratio test. In addition to that I am impressed by the fact that when the ceiling was descending in 1965 the Treasury found it appropriate to extend the period in which the ceiling would descend.

Because of the extension, the ceiling is not going to descend on everybody at the same time. Therefore, the impact is spread out over time, which perhaps was the result of an interesting tactical approach. Perhaps we need, if we agree that that is an unfortunate constraint, to get together to make the case for removal.

Now, may I have two minutes for rejoinder, Professor Bierman?

In view of the fact that the specifics were not made as to what this cruel and unusual punishment which I have been relieved of were made, I can only say that we shall meet in the footnotes when the time comes. And, that's where I shall leave any references to specific points. I gather that it was a matter of pressure of time, rather than delicacy, that led Professor Bierman to leave out those details.

But his comment and also those very interesting ones of Professor Baumol lead me to a line of distinction which I think is useful to have made explicit to this and other groups.

There are two approaches in economics, both of which are intellectually satisfying and I am sure socially useful to those who choose one or the other.

There are those who build the mathematical models of how behavior would occur if those who make decisions follow the line of reasoning of the model builders and accept their assumptions. To an increasing extent economists are intrigued with the mathematical models.

In contrast there are those who are more concerned with trying to appraise how decisions are made and advise public policy taking account of the facts.

Both Professor Bierman and Professor Baumol have indicated approaches by which, if there were flexibility in investment between the purchase of debt and the purchase of equity, an investor could reach a certain balance that would maximize an investment. But, in point of fact, do investors switch from one to the other or do we still have compartmentalization in the money market?

Some of the discussion here reminds me of an incident which occurred many years ago when a very eminent economist in a very eminent institution made a prediction that, if a certain policy was followed for a year, certain dire results would occur.

The policy was followed. The results did not occur. And an unfriendly reporter who remembered the prediction came back after the year was over and said, "Professor, does your prediction not disprove the validity of economic analysis?" The Professor, with a confident arrogance that is enviable though hardly useful said, "Not at all. If the American people had understood economics, it would have occurred."

In terms of the value of economics for public policy, I am, shall I say, on somewhat the other side from that approach to economics which relies on models and is contemptuous of facts.

Comment by Professor David McCord Wright, Department of Economics, University of Georgia: This excellent discussion has provided me with lots of points on which I would like to ask questions, but I'll cut it down to one.

I would like to ask Professor Hogan if his questionnaire distinguished between projects already begun and projects merely contemplated? I mean by that that once you started over Niagara Falls it might be hard to pull out but, if he had asked how many not yet started but contemplated projects had been canceled, that might have produced a much different result. I wonder if that was taken into consideration.

Professor Hogan: The purpose here was to find out what effect the suspension of the credit would have on the inflation that was under way at the time. A project of a long-term nature that had not been started wouldn't have any effect on inflation. No money would be spent on that probably for several years in advance.

I was concerned in this questionnaire to find out how much spending would be curtailed immediately to combat the inflationary trend that was under way. That was the purpose of it.

Now, a project that would have been deferred and which would not have resulted in an expenditure for another year was not under consideration.

Our purpose was to find out whether we curtailed spending now.

Professor Wright: But they don't all start at the same time.

Professor Hogan: No.

Professor Wright: Of course, if you talk as of the moment the tax is imposed, it might not affect the new plant in construction, still it would seem to me that if you are not limiting yourself to instant results, and talk of plans over three months, there might be a margin of contemplated investment that might have been stopped.

Professor Hogan: This is a possibility.

Professor Karl W. Roskamp, Wayne State University: Both speakers have discussed the effects of income taxes on risk taking in investment. A number of economists have argued that if the income tax laws provide a loss offset provision, which makes the government a partner in gains as well as in losses, the effects of income taxation on investment would not be so unfavorable. I have two questions.

First—How does business look at the loss offset provision? Second, what changes in these, if any, are considered desirable to enhance the flow of risk capital?

Mr. Tyson: First, I should say that I do not consider the government a partner in my business just because they take half of what I get. It is a reluctant giving, shall I say.

There is one way, very obviously, to avoid the payment of tax and that is not to make any money. If you don't have any profit, you don't have to pay it. I would, however, hate to be a part of a profitless enterprise system.

Now, as to the offset of loss operations, it fits right into that package because you have only the net of profits after losses out of which to pay taxes. Therefore, it is a little bit ridiculous, in my mind, to consider that you should ignore losses in paying taxes and you should only pay on the profits.

Being in business in the United States and in foreign countries also, we feel there are some who believe that you should pay anywhere up to 100 percent on your profit but we, in this country, haven't gotten quite that foolish yet and I don't believe we will.

There was another part to your question that I think I have missed.

Professor Roskamp: The second part was: What changes in the loss offset provision, if any, does business consider deirable to enhance the flow of risk capital?

Mr. Tyson: Of course, there are many changes that each of us would make if we were privileged with regard to the writing of the tax laws. I think that the taxing of capital gains is a deterrent to capital flow. I think one of the most unrealistic things that we have in our tax law is the depreciation policy.

We have talked at length about the investment credit, which is an important part of the present law and I subscribe to one of the statements that was made that business did not wrap its arms around it when it was proposed, but people seem to forget very easily that the investment credit was a substitute for realistic depreciation, which is the recovery of the capital that is consumed, and not just the dollars that were paid for it in the past.

I happen to believe that the only true depreciation policy is one which recognizes erosion of the monetary unit. It was not possible, perhaps not practical to think that that could be accomplished, and the investment credit was accepted as a compromise by the business community. This is why you have it on the books today, or did have it, I should say, before it was suspended and we now talk about suspending the suspension.

But those are two areas which, in my judgment, are extremely important in considering the flow of capital funds.

Professor Smith: Might I just add to that that I am skeptical as to the value of any sweeping generalization or categorical statement about the importance of the tax treatment of losses. It depends on the type of investment.

Take one extreme, a proposal for a capital investment that will save so many man-years in a known way in an existing assembly line for instance. Now, there it is a matter of return with virtually no conceivable likelihood of loss. That's the one extreme.

The other extreme is a merchandising of a new product where the statistics show that only one out of five products will make a go of the proposition.

If it's the latter sort of a situation, then the loss deduction becomes of very considerable significance. I am very skeptical about a sweeping generalization.

Take another instance where there is a certainty of loss for several years as in a cable television company where, while they are getting their subscription lists set up, it will take several years of losses. Subchapter S is very useful for that sort of venture because the stockholders get the immediate deduction.

Professor Eli Schwartz, Lehigh University: I address my question to Professor Bierman. Mostly I have heard favorable comments about the 7 percent investment credit. However, let's admit that this credit is a form of tax reduction and that the reduction could be spread through the economy in some other way. For example, we could reduce, perhaps, the total corporate income tax rate, the overall rate, one or two percentage points.

Now, some firms invest in heavy capital, others invest in inventory and financial assets. Some firms are financial intermediaries. Some sell goods at the retail or the wholesale level. We presume, now that we have gotten past Adam Smith, that all of these activities are considered productive to the general economy.

Why single out the firms that are capital intensive for a tax benefit? Why wouldn't it be fair and more equitable to reduce the overall rate one or two percentage points across the line?

Professor Bierman: I might say that currently the firms that are capital intensive are not singled out for benefit. The firms that use capital expenditures in the form of advertising and research and development are singled out for special treatment since these expenditures may be expensed when they are incurred, even though their benefits may be long run.

Secondly, I am personally not in favor of the investment credit as a way of stimulating investment because it, combined with accelerated depreciation, guideline lives, reserve ratio tests, treatment of salvage, and retirement treatments are much too complex for the average academic person, and much too complex for the average businessman.

I will go along with an alternative scheme, some way of simplifying the tax treatment of investments. The cash outlay is at time of investment, at least for a large, wide segment of investments. I personally think that we could ease into a situation of allowing immediate expensing of that expenditure for tax purposes.

Now, there are some drawbacks in terms of this policy possibly being countercyclical effects. I am aware of these difficulties but just let me point out one thing. If we are dealing with investments of a life of say eight years, it is not clear as to whether there would be a net cost to the government of such a treatment. What I am thinking of is that one can substitute immediate expensing for the whole gamut of gifts, allowances, and so forth, that are currently in effect, that are much more complex. The cost of compliance is high, the confusion is great.

This is my suggestion. Place investments on an equal, comparable basis to advertising.

Professor Schwartz: Does not the accumulation of inventory stocks or the increase of working capital require you to use more capital and this is also true for an increase of financial assets for a bank or other financial intermediary?

Professor Bierman: That's correct. Now, if you want to make it more all-encompassing and work it around to the investment in inventory, fine.

Professor Schwartz: No, I am suggesting a lower tax rate for everyone.

Professor Bierman: Let me just say that one would assume that there is more risk associated with a long-term investment, that is, with an investment in a long-lived asset. I criticized the risk statements of U.S. Steel about the erosion of the dollar, but I am not entirely lacking in sympathy.

They have a fear that if they depreciate this asset over 50 years the amount of the depreciation taken for tax purposes 30 years from now will be worth much less than a dollar today in terms of purchasing power.

I would like to relieve that fear somewhat, remove or at least reduce one risk. This is done currently by an initial depreciation write-off, by an investment credit, and by the shortening of lives. I think these matters are extremely complex, and it is difficult for the average businessman to understand the economic importance of them.

Professor Baumol: But there can be a very good economic basis on which one might favor an investment tax credit over a reduction in the corporate income tax, depending on the nature of the social objectives.

It is very clear that any special tax provision has a distorting effect on the market but distortion is not necessarily bad. A rational decision to favor the tax credit would imply that we believe that the market without certain incentives does not produce as rapid a rate of growth as is required by the national purpose, whatever that may mean.

In other words, we may decide that we should give business special payments, special bonuses for their contributions to growth. Of course, this would require a much more refined investment tax credit arrangement than we have now. It may be entirely rational to conclude that the market equilibrium would by itself provide such and such a rate of growth but that for military reasons or a variety of other reasons we would like the economy to grow more quickly than that and our incentive structure should be changed accordingly.

Question: But you are assuming the corporations actually pay the taxes that are levied against them?

Professor Baumol: Oh, no, even if there is shifting it need not matter. This is the point that I made before. For example, if the shifting of the tax credit involves a reduction in prices, presumably it will produce an increase in sales. It may result in expansion just as much as if the sum went into profits.

Mr. Robert Ulin, Mobil Oil Corporation: I would like to ask Professor Smith, whether he has a specific idea about the form of a penalty tax on additional direct foreign investment. Are you referring to taxation of income as earned from the additional investments or a variant of the interest equalization tax, or whatever you would like to say about that?

Professor Smith: I am opposed to discriminatory tax against foreign investment because I think the maintenance of the flow of income, both direct and associated with foreign investment, is extremely important for our balance of payments.

My comments at the end were, I am sure, too brief. What I am greatly concerned about are the proposed Treasury regulations on section 482 involving the allocation of income between the United States and foreign countries. What is proposed would involve a disallowance of expenses here which, I am absolutely certain, will not be allowed as expenses in most other industrial countries and in most of the underdeveloped countries. The net result will be that the total tax burden on foreign investment will be greater than that on domestic investment, greater than that on indigenous investment in the foreign countries and greater than that on investments in other industrial countries abroad.

I think the competition is tough enough as it is and United

States business should not be put at a tax disadvantage in trying to maintain its competitive share of income from abroad.

My paper elaborates on that somewhat.

Professor Oswald H. Brownlee, Chairman, Department of Economics, University of Minnesota: I would like to address my question to Mr. Bierman. The suggestion was made, and I think on the surface it sounds very good, that all assets be permitted to be written off in the first year for depreciation purposes.

As we are quite aware, the existing tax laws favor short-lived assets in comparison with long-lived assets. However, I think one thing that was neglected is that, if you expense the assets in the year in which they are purchased at, let's say, 50 percent, they can then be sold and subjected to the capital gains tax, which is only 25 percent. (The effective rate is probably 7 or 8 percent instead of 25 percent.)

Therefore, it would be possible for us to get overinvestment in capital equipment in assets of all lives rather than under-investment in long-lived assets, as we have at the present time.

An alternative possibility is to make the discounted value of depreciation the same, regardless of the life of the asset, as this would remove the discrimination against long-lived assets in comparison with short-lived assets and would also not subject the investment to the current income tax or give it credit at the current income tax rate and then bring the income or its effective income back at the capital gains tax.

What I mean is as follows:

Say you have a 20-year asset. Let's permit the person to write off twice as much as the purchase price, with a ten-year asset, say, 1.4 times as much, with a two-year asset, 1.1 times.

Professor Bierman: Relative to the first point, I certainly would not be in favor of allowing capital gains treatment of any resulting gain and, as most of the audience is aware, this is not currently allowed.

The reference is to my statement that the complexities of the changing tax code are hard to keep track of. We might plug a loophole, but in plugging that loophole the number of complexities introduced may be numerous and defy inter-pretation.

The second point was to make the present value of depreciation of the various lived assets equal, thereby eliminating one distortion. Of course, it introduces a bias in favor of long-lived assets, all things being equal. Though I must confess that an immediate write-off would also make the present value of the depreciation equal and thus create a distortion of a type, thus my suggestion introduces a type of distortion.

There is obviously no one answer here that is going to satisfy everyone. I will suggest the following.

If we assume an asset is supplying reasonably equal service potentials or cash flows throughout its life, or even an asset that is decreasing slightly in terms of service potentials or cash flow throughout its life, then any theoretically correct method of depreciation would not look at all like our accelerated depreciation (sum of the years digits, double declining balance or any other of the commonly used methods). Among other things, I would like to reduce confusion and make the investment analysis more simple.

You might be interested in the fact that when a commission in England studied this problem, they came up with the conclusion that it didn't make much sense to pass a law allowing accelerated depreciation because the methods of investment analysis used by the business community were so naive they wouldn't incorporate the tax savings into the analysis. This is consistent with what Professor Smith said before.

Now, I don't accept this in terms of long-run objectives, but it is still true that many U.S. firms do not use accelerated depreciation despite the basic advantage to them. The classic case is AT&T.

But even going beyond regulated industry, certainly there are many firms that are not using the accelerated methods of depreciation, not taking advantage of something that, to most of us, is an obvious tax advantage.

Professor Baumol: I'd like to ask one question of Father Hogan and have one small point of disagreement with him, if he will excuse me.

The point on which I would like to disagree is the implication that the firms which are now contributing to the control of pollution are making a net social contribution. What has really happened is that they have stopped beating their wives.

Heretofore they have been imposing social costs on the

economy and now we want to pay them for ceasing to do so.

This is not simply a matter of ethics. It is a very important matter of economic efficiency. That is, we want it to be more expensive to drive a car, because a car pollutes the atmosphere, as a means to discourage that activity. We want those who impose social costs to pay for them and we don't want to pass the cost on to the community in general.

The question I wanted to ask was on your survey. Since it apparently shows that elimination or suspension of the tax credit had little effect, would you guess that re-imposition of the tax credit would also have very little effect?

Professor Hogan: May I address myself to the first point.

It is true that some companies have been polluting the air and water for a number of years and, although some effort was made to cut down on pollution it has persisted to a limited extent. Thus, we have an historical situation and in this context, because of the more stringent regulations that are imposed year after year, very large capital outlays are suddenly necessary which had never been required before. Previously, the pollution of air and water had been accepted as a sort of necessary evil connected with certain types of manufacturing. Granted this should not have been, the historical fact is that it was.

The installation of air and water pollution controls can be a decided burden to a company, particularly if the company is a marginal operation. This burden can be a severe shock and that is why I think that, under these circumstances, the companies should be given some tax relief itself, if they make this contribution to the common good.

It is quite different if someone starts in business today, for air and water pollution controls are recognized as a distinct cost of construction in a plant.

Now, on the other question, I would say this. We were looking to see what immediate effect this had as a short-run tool and, as a short-run tool, the conclusion seems to be it was not too effective. However, as a long-run tool, I think that it would have cut down on capital spending to some extent and, therefore, the restoration of it will keep capital spending going in the long run.

PART II

PART II

REVIEW OF OUR EXPERIENCE IN ADMINISTERING FISCAL POLICY*

PAUL W. McCRACKEN

IGH ON THE list of deficiencies which economists share with Americans generally is inattention to the lessons of history. While we use time series and other raw material of experience prodigiously, we are not much inclined to read the minutes of earlier meetings in order to gain some historical perspective about how we got to where we are. It is, therefore, in order for us to explore in this symposium the record of our experience with the operation of economic policy.

As we examine this record, one conclusion stands out sharply. Fiscal and monetary policies have themselves been a major source of erratic movements in the economy, and the first requirement for improving our economic performance is that these policies themselves be operated in a more evenhanded and steady manner. Far from automating fiscal policy, this view of the problem will, if it is correct, require considerably more sophistication and precision than we have yet applied to the task.

Economic Instability in Historical Perspective

The prevailing concept about the nature of the problem of

---

*Mark Riedy was most helpful in assembling materials for this paper.

economic instability is itself a manifestation of our disinclination to examine history. We have tended to assume that ours is an economy with strong indigenous tendencies to ricochet from inflation to unemployment unless these are neutralized by stabilizing economic policies. Our strategy, then, must be for these policies to detect whether the economy is starting to zig or to zag, and then to push vigorously in the other direction.

There is a good deal of historical evidence to suggest that this conception of the nature of the problem is close to being 180 degrees off course. It would be more in accord with the evidence of history to say that we have had an economy with an impressive capacity to follow a course of vigorous and orderly expansion—except when it has been derailed by a miscarriage of economic policy. Suppose that we explore this a bit to see whether it seems to square with the facts of history.

For several reasons it is useful here to begin with the pre-1929 era, specifically the four decades from 1889 to 1929. Annual data are reasonably available. Moreover, the period has certain natural advantages for our point. We did not even have a central banking system for two-thirds of these years. During most of these four decades the federal budget was equal in magnitude to about 3 percent of GNP, so its inherent capacity to keep an erratic economy on a short leash would have been severely limited. In any case the concept of fiscal policy had not even been invented at this time. Thus we have here a segment of history during which we should be able to observe the private economy in the raw before the instruments of economic stabilization were really available to exert their soothing effects on its natural instability.

The National Bureau of Economic Research has decreed that there were 12 identifiable cyclical swings in this span of four decades. And there were eight years during which real output fell below that of the previous year.[1] When we examine the data more closely, however, we discover some interesting things. The median decline for the recedence years was only 2.6 percent in real output. In eight of the 12 recessions real output

---

[1] Cf. *Long-term Economic Growth, 1860-1965* (Washington, D. C.: Bureau of the Census, 1966), pp. 166-67.

in the year containing the low point of the recession was higher than that for the year containing the previous peak.

The four more serious recessions were 1894, 1908, 1914, and 1921. The recession of 1908 was clearly associated with a major monetary panic, and the collapse of 1921 arose out of an overly expansionist set of policies through 1919, followed in 1920 by a drastic reversal of both monetary and fiscal policies. The $13.7 billion swing from a large deficit in FY 1919 to a small surplus in FY 1920 was equal to 16 percent of GNP in 1919 (the equivalent of a $120 billion year-to-year restrictive budgetary swing today). And in three moves the Federal Reserve pushed the discount rate to an all-time high of 7 percent by mid-1920, forcing a 5.2 percent contraction in the money supply from mid-1920 to mid-1921. The remarkable thing here is not that there was a 1921 recession but that our economic system even survived this massive fiscal and monetary whipsaw.

Here clearly what we are observing is not an economy with some endemic case of the shakes, inherently tending to dash from the cellar to the penthouse. It is a record of surprisingly orderly and sustained expansion, except when our foot was pressed too heavily on the accelerator or on the brakes and often in quick succession.

The final decade of this period, 1922 to 1929, is particularly instructive here. Indeed, it is one of the ironies of history that this vastly underrated economic performance tends so often to be characterized as the era that landed us in the ditch of the Great Depression. Actually it was a period that lived up well to Section 2 of the Employment Act. Real output rose at the average rate of 4.7 percent per year, and each year saw a rise. The price level was steady. And the unemployment rate averaged 3.6 percent.

This good economic performance was no accident. The money supply rose quite steadily at the average rate of 5.1 percent per year, and fiscal policy was also turning in an impressive performance. The full-employment surplus—the difference between federal outlays and the receipts that the revenue system would produce at full employment—for fiscal years 1923 to 1930 apparently ranged from a low of about $0.7 billion in 1926 and 1929 to a high of just under $1 billion in 1930.

Thus this calibration of fiscal policy, which is, of course, analytically superior to actual surpluses as a measure of fiscal policy, shows a remarkable stability with a full employment surplus of somewhat less than 1 percent of GNP during this period.

Though it has required about three decades to get the point in focus, we do now see that the Great Depression itself was also the result, particularly in the critical 1931 to 1933 phase, of our doing things wrong in the field of public policy virtually whenever there was an opportunity to do so. And we also now see that the catastrophe had nothing to do with any inherent

Full-Employment Surpluses, 1923-30
(In billions)

Fiscal Year	Surplus
1923	$0.7
1924	0.8
1925	0.7
1926	0.6
1927	1.0
1928	1.0
1929	0.7
1930	0.9

Source: Estimates for potential GNP were interpolated from James W. Knowles, "The Potential Economic Growth of the United States," Joint Economic Committee, 86th Congress, 2d Session, 1960, p. 37. Annual Commerce estimates of GNP were converted to quarterly data using the quarterly pattern of Harold Barger, *Outlay and Income in the United States, 1921 to 1928* (New York: National Bureau of Economic Research, 1942), pp. 114-19. The ratio of actual GNP to potential was then applied to each fiscal year's revenues. This figure minus actual expenditures is the derived full-employment surplus estimate. The estimates are based on the administrative budget.

or natural tendency of our economic system to operate at underemployment levels. What we had here was a massive monetary bloodletting. By 1933 the full-employment money supply would have been roughly 50 percent above actual levels, and our zeal for economic masochism had enabled us to accomplish the extraordinary feat of committing financial genocide against 40 percent of our banks. We had 25,000 banks in 1929, and we emerged in 1933 with about 15,000.

Fiscal policy was also afflicted with its full share of gremlins in this period. The full-employment surplus moved from a deficit to a modest surplus in the critical 1932-33 period, a "wrong" swing of close to 2 percent of GNP. And the swing in the full-employment surplus from a deficit of roughly $2.5 billion in 1936 to a surplus of less than $1 billion in 1937 (a perverse swing equal to about 4 percent of GNP) was certainly a major source of the downturn in 1937 that began before we had regained full employment—a downturn of great conceptual significance because it raised questions about the ability of our economy to sustain reasonably full employment.

The long-sustained period of abnormally high unemployment that began in 1957 is, of course, another illustration of an aberration in our economic performance whose sources can be traced to economic policy. The glacial pace of monetary expansion from 1956 through 1959, excluding a brief interlude early in 1958, was certainly a major factor. The money supply from the end of 1955 to the end of 1959 was allowed to increase at the rate of 3.1 percent per year, considerably short of that required for the economy to keep on a growth path consistent with reasonably full utilization of our productive resources.

It was here, of course, that fiscal policy also was allowed to wander off course in a major way. In the recedence phase fiscal policy actually was working well. The full-employment surplus was declining rapidly to a $1-$2 billion level by the end of 1958, and this contributed to the brevity of the decline and the strong subsequent upswing. At this point things went awry. The full-employment surplus then rose from this $1-$2 billion annual rate at the end of 1958 to the $14 billion zone two years later. Subjected to these fiscal and monetary drags, the economy faltered in 1960 before it achieved full employment. The administration's failure to provide leadership for a 1958 tax reduction cost the economy another recession and the Republican party the White House in 1960.

So much for ancient history. Fortunately in recent years, some of you may feel, the forces of darkness that produced these aberrant results have been dispersed, and with the "new economics" we have ushered in an age of enlightenment. Since 1961, we have been told, about as often in lyric poetry as in prose, that the economic performance has been truly remarkable. Now it has been a better performance than we saw in the

1950s. From 1960 to 1966 real output grew at the average annual rate of 4.8 percent per year—quite impressive for an economy whose long-run growth rate has been about 3.5 percent. Moreover, there has been no recession since 1961, though the status of this sentence has been a bit rickety recently. And we had a major tax decrease in 1964 that clearly helped the economy to regain full employment somewhat over a year later.

The "New Economics"

Now it is not easy to gain perspective on the new economics. For one thing the precise substantive content of the phrase is astonishingly difficult to identify. There is certainly very little in its literature about objectives of economic policy that is new. Let me quote a sentence: "Government must use all practicable means to promote high levels of production and employment, and to contribute toward achieving an expanding and widely-shared national income earned in dollars of stable buying power." The author of this sentence, which might have come even from Gotham's junior senator, was actually a spokesman more benevolently disposed toward this administration—namely, the last Republican President in his 1957 Economic Report.

Nor have there been major innovations in the instruments of economic policy. The guidelines were a logical extension of increasing official attention before 1962 to the wage-price problem, but they seem to have a tenuous hold on official affection now in any case. There was a large tax reduction in 1964 that was needed and effective, equal in magnitude to 2.1 percent of 1965's GNP, the year in which the full reduction became effective. We have had, however, other tax cuts of similar relative magnitude. A decade earlier the $7.4 billion tax reduction was equal to 2.0 percent of 1954's GNP, and it was in the face of a substantial deficit in the budget. Moreover, it was made with the economic situation in mind—this according to no less a "new economist" than Secretary of the Treasury Humphrey. Indeed, one of the best performances in tax reductions, or for the fiscal policy generally, was in the mid-1920s when in three steps the revenue producing capability of the federal tax structure was reduced by $1.6 billion. This was equal again to roughly 2 percent of GNP, and the full-employment surplus was kept remarkably steady.[2]

Perhaps the main basis for claiming that our capacity to execute policy has improved dramatically in recent years is simply that the performance of the economy has been so much better. This better performance must mean that policies have also been different and better. Undoubtedly our policy capabilities have improved. Hopefully we learn a few things as we go along. What needs far more critical evaluation, however, is precisely this basic premise that our performance in recent years has been so superior that it is out of context with our historical experience. This is not so obvious as it may seem. The average annual rate of growth in the 1920s was equal to that since 1960—4¾ percent per year in both cases. And we did at least that well for a period that was twice as long from 1895 to 1907 both cyclical peak years.

The real point here, however, is something more fundamental than a crude comparison of growth rates. That the growth capability of the economy was going to be unusually high in the 1960s was determined less by the new economics than by the birth statistics following the war that made a rapid subsequent rise in the labor force ineluctably certain. We

Average Annual Increase in the Labor Force

Period	Number
1950-1960	807,100
1960-1965	1,046,000
1965-1975*	1,529,000

*Based on projections.
Source: Department of Labor

are now in a period when the annual increments to the labor force are almost double their numbers in the 1950s, and there is some evidence that the rate of growth in productivity is also favorably affected by the higher rate of growth in output made possible by the more rapidly enlarging labor force.[3] The test of policy is how the economy operated relative to this more

---

[2] Annual Report, Secretary of the Treasury, Fiscal Year 1926, p. 24.
[3] Cf. Nicholas Kaldor, *Causes of the Slow Rate of Economic Growth of the United Kingdom* (Cambridge: 1966).

rapidly rising potential. And here the record since 1960 is simply not superior. In the low quarter of 1961, according to the Wharton School index of capacity, the economy's operating rate was 80.5 percent.[4] This was about the same as for the low point in 1958 and 1949, but it was below the 85.2 percent in the third quarter of 1954. The 1961 recession, in short, did not bring the economy's operating rate to a level unusually low by historical standards. In the year following the 1961 low point, the operating rate increased 6.2 percent. This is far less than the 13.4 percent improvement during the comparable period after the low point in 1958, or even the 9.4 percent after 1954. There was a 15.8 percent gain after the 1949 low quarter, but this was influenced by the Korean conflict. Moreover, after the first year's improvement of the operating rate into early 1962, there was no further gain until the second quarter of 1964. Or, to put it somewhat differently, after the low point in 1961 the economy required 16 quarters to accomplish a gain in its operating rate that required only 4 quarters in the post-1958 period—in both cases starting with about the same relative shortfall from par.

When we realize this, the absence of a recession during this period also takes on a somewhat different meaning. It arose in part out of the unusually long, drawn-out path of the return to full employment, and when full employment was finally achieved in the final quarter of 1965, some of the old problems again became visible.

Some may be tempted to conclude that those now in charge of policy are simply less expert practitioners of the new economics than their predecessors. This would do them a great injustice. Indeed, if we get through 1967 without a recedence of sufficient magnitude to be called a recession, and this is a distinct possibility, those now responsible for economic policy must be given at least as high marks as their predecessors—this because they have been navigating the narrow channel of a fully employed economy rather than operating out in open water.

Now the point of this quick tour of history is not to make the old days look good and the new days look bad. What does

---

[4] Release of March 8, 1967. This is the combined index of industrial and service capacity.

emerge is a good deal of evidence that departures from the full employment growth path have had their origins primarily in the domain of economic policy—and that this has had its manifestations in the era of the new economics as well as earlier.

Relationship Between Monetary and Fiscal Policy

While monetary policy extends beyond the scope of this paper, monetary and fiscal policy have a synergetic relationship with each other, and a few quick comments about the nature of this relationship may be in order. The usual conception is of two relatively separate and distinct instruments of policy, either of which can be used to achieve a certain effect on the level of business activity. We can, then, pursue an easier fiscal policy and a tighter monetary policy with a neutral effect on the level of business activity—making these off-setting adjustments in order to achieve certain subsidiary objectives such as a stronger balance of payments. The 1966 problem has occasionally been described as a condition where the brakes on the monetary wheel were set hard and the brakes on the fiscal wheel were not used—causing the economy to swerve.

Part of the trouble here is the use of some terms that have less precision than we often seem to realize. What do we mean by an easier or tighter fiscal policy? We now know that this must be measured by something other than the size of the actual surplus or deficit, because this with no fiscal actions at all can change simply as the level of business activity changes. We have solved this ambiguity in principle by the use of the full-employment surplus concept, expenditures less the receipts the tax system would produce at full employment. Apart from secular economic growth this changes only when the "fiscal functions" of the economy are changed—only when expenditure programs or tax rates are altered.

What, however, do we mean by an easier or tighter monetary policy? Clearly these phrases have little meaning if we are thinking in terms of whether credit markets are under pressure or whether interest rates are high or rising. We could, in that case, get "easier money" by a further decline in an already depressed demand for output, but this "easing" would be the harbinger of further economic deterioration rather than expansion. Or we could get "tighter money" in markets with accelerating demand, but "tight money" here would be an augury of further economic expansion rather than contraction.

Now, fortunately, there is a way out of this problem. It is opened up by the fact that the relationship between the money supply and GNP is fairly stable through time. During the last decade the ratio of the money supply to GNP averaged 43.3 percent, and only two (one being 1958) of the 11 years from 1956 to 1966 turned in a ratio deviating from this average by more than one percentage point.[5] If we calibrate monetary

GNP and the Money Supply
(Dollar amounts in billions)

Year	GNP	Money Supply* Amount	% GNP
1956	$419.2	$187.0	44.6
1957	441.1	191.1	43.3
1958	447.3	199.9	44.7
1959	483.7	207.9	43.0
1960	503.7	211.7	42.0
1961	520.1	221.1	42.5
1962	560.3	236.8	42.3
1963	590.5	·255.3	43.2
1964	631.7	275.8	43.7
1965	681.2	300.2	44.1
1966	739.6	321.2	43.4

*Time deposits are included. Each figure is the average of year-end figures bracketing the year and is based on seasonally adjusted data.
Source: Department of Commerce and Federal Reserve.

ease or tightness by the rate of monetary expansion, we have an unambiguous measure. A more rapid rate of monetary expansion is an easier monetary policy than a slower expansion. Thus monetary policy was tightening in 1966 because the rate of monetary expansion was reduced, not because interest rates were rising. And monetary policy became easier in the second half of 1965 because the rate of monetary expansion was allowed to accelerate, even though interest rates were also rising.

---

[5] Even on a first difference basis, quarterly changes in the money supply explain 44 percent of the changes in GNP.

Since the economy is not apt to stray far from the trail being blazed by the pace of monetary expansion, we must then be careful in our use of such trade-off terms as easier fiscal policy and tighter credit policy. A tighter monetary policy in the sense of a reduced pace of monetary expansion is apt to slow the economy even if fiscal policy is eased in the sense of reducing the full-employment surplus. Indeed, we could almost say that monetary policy establishes the level of business activity, and fiscal policy influences such financial matters as money and capital market conditions.

Now this is not to say that a change in fiscal policy has no effect on the level of business activity. It can help to activate an expansion or to cool off an overheated economy. The effect of, for example, an easier fiscal policy may work itself out through a reduced propensity to hold money, though the ongoing tolerances here are small, or it may force or enable the pursuit of a more rapid monetary expansion. In any case we do well to keep in mind the complex and subtle nature of the relationship between monetary policy and fiscal policy as we turn to the latter.

Fiscal Policy and Resource Allocation

It is well for us to remember, as we come to fiscal policy, that we want the fiscal operations of government to accomplish more for us than to help the economy pursue a stable growth path. Through government budgets we want to arrange for collectivized consumption and investment. And we also want these fiscal operations to redistribute the national income more equitably. Some of the most urgent work in budget policy must be concerned with these matters.

How can we assure that our budget procedures give effective expression to the preferences of people about the allocation of their incomes between public and private consumption and investment? There are major problems posed by our fiscal procedures here. For one thing the decision-making process that finally determines actual outlays is not subjected to the discipline of a total. Each appropriation bill must be decided "on its merits" and with whatever guesses and hunches can be mustered about what it will all probably add up to. Yet the aggregate of spending requests that have merit in themselves is bound to exceed a proper total. This is what the discipline of economics is all about.

It would, of course, be helpful if we could inject more marketplace disciplines into the public sector. Surface area devoted to streets, for example, might suffer from less excess demand if it were made less of a free good. The post office problem of junk mail is not that this mail is junky, a matter of definition, but that the post office offers to carry it at bargain-basement rates. Yet prospects here are not bright. New York could not muster political courage to meter water use even in the face of a crisis. If we cannot find ways to use market disciplines more, the case for an expansion of activities in the public sector is correspondingly weakened.

Government Taxes and Benefits Received, 1965
As a percentage of total income

Income Class	Taxes Paid	Benefits Received	Benefits Received Per Dollar of Taxes
Under $2,000	28.1%	109.0%	$3.88
$2,000-$2,999	26.7	65.0	2.43
$3,000-$3,999	29.7	46.0	1.55
$4,000-$4,999	29.1	33.7	1.16
$5,000-$5,999	29.4	29.5	1.00
$6,000-$7,499	28.5	25.4	.89
$7,500-$9,999	28.5	22.1	.78
$10,000-$14,999	30.6	20.0	.65
$15,000 and over	44.0	16.3	.37
Total	30.4	29.9	.98

Source: *Tax Burdens and Benefits of Government Expenditures by Income Class, 1961 and 1965* (New York: Tax Foundation, Inc., 1967).

The objective of redistributing income through the government's fiscal operations also needs to be brought into better balance and focus. What are the criteria for deciding how far the budget should attempt to go in income redistribution? Should we look only at the incidence of taxes, as is usually done, or should we look also at benefits received by income levels? While the total tax system does not seem to be highly progressive until we get to upper income groups, the total fiscal operations of government are redistributing the national income in favor of low income groups in a massive way. In 1965, according to one estimate, those with incomes under $2,000 received net benefits (benefits received less taxes paid) of 80 percent of their income. We can safely factor into decisions about tax policy other considerations than whether each tax change makes the tax system more progressive, secure in the knowledge that the nation's total fiscal system is heavily redistributing incomes toward lower income groups.

In these non-stabilization areas are to be found some of the least satisfactory aspects of budgetary policy, and it is good that they are now beginning to receive more attention. Our specific concern here, however, has to do with the contribution of fiscal policy to stable economic growth, and it is to this that we now turn.

Clearly the most fundamental contribution that fiscal policy can make to orderly and vigorous economic progress is that the budget itself pursue a more evenhanded and steady course. The blunt truth is that prospects for the budget are a major uncertainty in any appraisal of our economic prospects, and perverse swings in the budget have been an important source of instability. It is here that improvement must begin.

Budgetary Information and Concepts

First the flow of budget data is itself one of the more erratic and uncertain elements in our economic information system. Some of this is a simple matter of regular and prompt reporting. The *Mid-Year Budget Review,* for example, was not issued last year (a casualty of the late adjournment of the Congress), but it was also an unfortunate year to have no midterm reading on budget prospects. The government was able to publish in its March *Business Cycle Developments* a February figure for such a complex concept as labor costs per unit of output in all manufacturing, but for Defense Department obligations and military prime contract awards to U.S. business firms the latest figures it could produce were for January. The Defense Department's *Monthly Status of Funds* report was never issued for July and August last year, and the September issue straggled along in December. If a large corporation were to be that casual about its cooperation with the statistics-gathering agencies, it would rightly be considered in contempt of the public interest. Information on actual outlays is, of course, available more promptly and regularly, but these are not the fiscal data needed to form judgments about where the budget is going.[6]

We are fortunate that the Joint Economic Committee has just worked out an arrangement with the Bureau of the Budget whereby more frequent estimates of prospects for expenditures and revenues will become available regularly. Revised estimates will be made in July and again upon completion of congressional action on the budget. These, with the January budget message, will give us three regular readings on budget prospects each year, instead of one as in 1966. This is a major step forward.

Second, we need to review the structure and format of our budget information system, and the President has himself provided the leadership here with the appointment of his Commission on the Budget. What we must work toward is an interlocking data system that can give us better organized and more comprehensive information bearing on key policy questions. For one thing it must show the size of the whole federal fiscal operation. None of the three conventional budget concepts provides this today. For certain large operations only deficits or funds required beyond revolving receipts get into the conventional budget. The only approximation to this overview is Table 9, Appendix B, of the budget message, which has little visibility and gets little attention.

The system must also delineate more sharply the budgetary draft on money and capital markets. Obviously the deficits in none of the major present budget concepts do this. Sales of financial assets are really a means of financing the gap between revenues and expenditures, and they may have an even greater impact on credit markets than an outright sale of Treasury obligations. Treated as a negative expenditure, however, they show up as a reduced deficit. Moreover, the "economic deficit" should presumably also include seigniorage profits. And for intelligent allocative decisions the budget system should make

---

[6] Cf. Murray L. Weidenbaum, "The Federal Budget and the Outlook for Defense Spending," Economic Outlook Conference, University of Michigan, November, 1966.

clear the amount of resources devoted to various programs. This year's budget message seems to propose a decline in outlays for education, for example, but this is the effect of treating sales of financial assets as a negative expenditure, and an increase of about 15 percent in total outlays for education is actually proposed for FY 1968.

For the present the cash budget is probably the most analytically useful of the three budgets, contrary to the catechism usually imputed to economists, but a substantial advance toward a more comprehensive interlocking data system is now essential for better decision making in the arena of fiscal policy.

Third, we need a more explicit working concept of what constitutes the equilibrium relationship between receipts and expenditures that should be the navigation target for fiscal policy. In the always-balanced-budget era, we had such a guideline. It was crude, but it was definite. Indeed, on the whole it worked surprisingly well, and its definitiveness did inject a wholly desirable fiscal discipline into the budgetary process. A major limitation of the new fiscal policy is that we have never really replaced the old rule with anything. This has created problems of its own. Our conception of the problem as one of countering instability endemic to the private economy has led us to adopt a strategy of policy that is itself a major source of instability. Fiscal policy should, then, run to this side of the ship and then to the other, but often in this process it becomes itself the source of the ship's wallowing course.

The full-employment surplus gives us the guideline here that we need. It is consistent with the requirements of fiscal discipline and also with the new fiscal policy. Each proposed budget should be shown on a full employment as well as an actual basis. Moreover, our on-going operating rule should be that proposed expenditures balance with the receipts that our tax structure would produce at full employment. With such a rule a larger proportion of the years will have budgets consistent with stable economic growth than if we try to *ad hoc* our way along—playing it all by ear, leaning against the wind, judging each situation on its merits, and employing all of the other good phrases that imply a wisdom too profound to be limited by guidelines. History, as we have found, has written its own record of the results of this strategy, and it suggests that we should try for something better.

Now it should be clear that what is proposed here is no passive or automatic fiscal policy. If our expenditure and tax programs are to be managed so that the full-employment budget remains in close balance, a far more exacting and sophisticated management of fiscal policy will be required. We need to pass from the stage of the economic blacksmith to the narrower tolerances of economic engineering.

Finally, if the budget is to pursue a steadier course through time, the planning horizon for the budget must extend beyond the end of "next year." The nation has a right to ask of each administration that it lay out its present views about where the total budget ought to be going in the longer run. Each budget message should, therefore, include projections of total expenditures for five years ahead. Revenue recommendations should also be included that would be necessary for the budget, on a full-employment basis, to remain reasonably in balance. These projections would, of course, have to be remade annually to include the additional year, and projections for intervening years would have to be revised to take cognizance of each year's new developments that carry implications for future budgets. The process of working within a five-year framework clearly would make for a more orderly and disciplined budget operation than we now have. In an economy where annual federal fiscal transactions will push above $200 billion this year, we must have something beyond a series of annual budget battles to set the basic course of fiscal policy. The concept of a five-year horizon for the budget has already been endorsed by the Joint Economic Committee.[7] It is to be hoped that this will be another in their considerable array of contributions to an improved strategy of economic policy.

Promoting Economic Stability

Much of the discussion in recent years about strengthening the capability of policy to stabilize the economy has been in

---

[7] *The Federal Budget as an Economic Document*, Joint Economic Committee, 88th Congress, 1st Session, 1963, p. 11. The Committee restates its support for this proposal in its current report. Cf., 1967 Joint Economic Report, 90th Congress, 1st Session, 1967, p. 12.

terms of introducing greater flexibility—that is, giving the President limited power over tax rates. These proposals have merit, and in some of my prose support is to be found for them. Most of the important ones would require approval of the Congress, however, and the Congress has seemed fully capable of restraining its enthusiasm about these suggestions. Moreover, the theory of strategy often implied here is that the primary task of policy is to dash about quelling uprisings whose origins are in the private economy. This is based on a faulty premise, and it is too crude and primitive a strategy for the modern economy.

Since a major source of departures from the path of vigorous and orderly growth and reasonably full employment has been the fitful and spasmodic behavior of fiscal and monetary policies, the most fundamental requirement for orderly movement along the full-employment growth path is that fiscal and monetary policies themselves pursue a more steadfast course. It is here that the greatest gains are to be had, and fortunately this does not involve colliding with any great constitutional issues such as the doctrine of the separation of powers. Moreover, it is worth repeating that this is not a recommendation for abdication to automaticity. It is a call for learning to operate these instruments of policy with more sophistication and exactitude, and within substantially narrower tolerances than in the past.

If we can keep expenditures in close balance with revenues that the tax system will generate at full employment, and if the course of monetary expansion also moves more steadily along the full employment growth path, we can reasonably expect that the economy will come even closer to a course broadly consistent with utilizing all of our "plans, functions, and resources . . . to promote maximum employment, production, and purchasing power."

ECONOMIC FORECASTING AS A BASIS FOR FISCAL POLICY DECISIONS

SOLOMON FABRICANT

OUR QUESTION is whether forecasting can be of help in making fiscal and other economic policy decisions. I think the answer is in the affirmative. Despite all its limitations—and they are serious—forecasting can help, and in fact is helping, to make economic policy decisions somewhat better than they would be without its assistance.

You will have noticed that I tried to be cautious in wording this conclusion. Nevertheless, it may still seem like a foolhardy statement to make at a time when there are so many differences of opinion on the drift of the economy and concern over the wisdom of current economic policy. Yet I think the statement can be justified. Indeed, the present controversy reflects an awareness and anxiety that might reasonably be viewed as evidence in support of the statement. If it were not for the forecasting going on—mixed though the results are—the country would be less sensitive to the dangers ahead. There might be more serious talk, or more than just talk, about raising taxes. The probability of a recession would be greater.

Let us venture further. Forecasting is helpful, but not as much as it could be even within its present limitations. In many forecasts insufficient use is made of available knowledge.

Yet at the same time, more knowledge is implied than anyone now possesses.

I hasten to emphasize, at the cost of repetition, that even at its best forecasting has severe limitations. Forecasts cannot and never will be as helpful as we would like. But they could be, and I believe would be, much more helpful if the current flow of information and the scientific basis of forecasting were to be improved. There is some progress in this respect, but it is not fast enough. A stepped-up rate of investment would yield a high rate of return. It ought to be made.

Patterns and Indicators of Cyclical Change

Let me begin to spell out what I have just put very briefly by assuring the skeptics that economic forecasting is not entirely a matter of hunch. There is plenty of need for hunch in making judgments on the economic outlook, but a responsible judgment will rest also on tested knowledge of how the economy operates. There is such tested knowlege. It is real, and though limited it is not negligible.

By subjecting experience to analysis, economists have discovered patterns of long- and short-term change in economic life, and have confirmed what they learned from one sample of experience by analyses of the information for other periods and other countries. We now know—it has become an "obvious" fact—that economic growth proceeds at an uneven pace and that the sequence of events along the path of economic growth is sufficiently repetitive so that we may properly speak of the typical features of a business-cycle expansion or contraction. More specifically, some economic series usually turn down before a peak is reached in general business, and some turn down afterwards. During a business revival there is a similar sequence in which certain economic series turn up before the bottom is reached and some turn up afterwards. The classification of indicators of business expansion and contraction that appears monthly in the Department of Commerce's *Business Cycle Developments*—the leaders, the roughly coincident indicators, and the laggards—is not arbitrary or speculative. The categories are derived from experience. The evidence for the classification is documented in a long series of studies, of which the recently published National Bureau volume by Geoffrey H. Moore and Julius Shiskin is the latest.

These and other systematic patterns of change are useful in formulating expectations about the future. This is so even though the patterns are never perfectly regular, and even when we do not know just why the patterns take the form they do. The knowledge derived from patterns is greater, however, and can be applied more confidently, when there is some understanding of the connections among the events that make up the patterns. Indeed, patterns inevitably stimulate efforts to devise explanations, and economists have long been engaged in this kind of enterprise. They have had some success in learning why one event usually follows another. They know better than before, to refer to an example central to the subject of the present symposium, not only how decisions to invest change during business cycles, but why.

In their analyses further, economists have not neglected to consider systematic and other changes in typical patterns. Study of these changes is an essential step in their tests of the stability of the patterns. In these studies, we have learned something of the extent and manner of variation among business cycles.

To our knowledge of the resemblances that have persisted from one business-cycle generation to another, we are adding an understanding of the kinds of changes that have taken place between generations. The postwar business cycle is different from the prewar, though not as different as some people are prone to assume. And economists are identifying some of the changes in the banking system and our other economic institutions that account for this evolution.

We know something also of the variation caused by the episodic factors that affect business cycles. Each business cycle has its own peculiar characteristics as well as its resemblances to others of its generation and species. These peculiarities are important. To provide information for making sensible policy decisions at any particular time, the forecaster must try to estimate not simply the typical course of events—what may be expected for the species on the average—or even the course of events to be expected in the average postwar business cycle. He must try to estimate the particular course of events that will characterize the business cycle with which he is immediately concerned, the current cycle. Knowledge of the typical course of events and of its evolution is useful for this purpose but it is not sufficient.

"Special" factors are difficult to deal with, almost by definition. Yet even with regard to these, forecasters are not entirely helpless. While the appearance of these factors is usually difficult to predict, economists can often say something about the direction of their effects, should they appear, and sometimes even a bit more. An obvious example is the outbreak of a war, or of a peace. Not all economists failed to see that the pent-up demand for civilian goods, backed by large and highly liquid funds in the hands of buyers, would sustain consumer demand and help to check the recession that followed the severe drop in federal expenditures in 1945.

Interpreting Business Cycle Indicators

I have been saying that "we" know something about the features of business cycles and that this helps "us" to analyze current business conditions. These words need to be qualified. The knowledge is not as widely diffused as it ought to be, even among those who venture to talk publicly about the business situation. Not everyone has the knowledge, or if he has it, does not fully appreciate its significance for evaluating current developments. This is one reason why opinions differ about the business situation today.

A rather common error is to read a decline in the leading indicators as evidence of recession, as some people have been doing for months now. Such a decline does signal the possibility of trouble ahead. The more pervasive, the more persistent, and the steeper the declines among the leading indicators—orders for equipment, profit margins, and industrial material prices, for example—the greater is the probability of trouble. But the threat need not necessarily be followed by a recession and the chances that it will can be reduced if appropriate action is taken by government. The point is that a recession is not defined by a decline in the leading indicators alone. Not until aggregate production, employment, and other roughly coinciding indicators are also falling, can one venture to say that a recession may be under way. And not until these declines—in both leading and coinciding indicators—have persisted long enough to be joined by the lagging indicators can we begin to be sure that it is.

At the present time, which means as of March or even February, because few of the statistics are up to date, all the leading indicators listed in the current *Business Cycle Developments* are below their peaks. Some are down quite sharply. Also, except for housing permits and starts, the stock market, and one or two other series, all seem still to be falling. But most of the roughly coincident series are on a plateau or still rising, with the exception of industrial production. Indeed, with this exception, their levels are at historic highs. And the only lagging indicator not still rising is the series on bank rates charged on short-term business loans. I would judge that we may be very close to being in a recession, but we are not in one yet.

A tendency to see recessions before they have actually appeared stems also from the fact that industrial experience typically becomes rather mixed well before a peak has been reached. Indeed, an expansion is most widely diffused as a rule, some six or 12 months before the highest stage of the business cycle. The proportion of industries experiencing a rise in output, sales, employment, and incomes, then, is typically falling, and the scope of the expansion narrowing as the peak is approached. Industries here and there—still only a minority, to be sure, but a growing minority—stop rising and start to decline. More and more men experience poorer business in their own industries, and they hear complaints of like experience from more and more of their business acquaintances. During the past 14 months, for example, the percentage of nonagricultural industries with rising employment (measured by change over the preceding six-month span) fell pretty steadily from about 95 percent early in 1966 to a level in January, 1967 (the most recent month available) of about 70 percent. A similar measure of change in output for the industries covered by the FRB index of industrial production was 100 percent in February, 1966, 75 percent in July, and under 40 percent in January, 1967.

Profits, Costs, and Investment

Economists will avoid the elementary errors I have just described. But even they may err in their judgment of the business situation when they fail to appreciate or use information supplied by certain cyclical changes to which they should be alert.

My example is again from the sphere of business investment. It is an old story that the incentive to invest in plant and equipment depends on the cost of plant and equipment, the cost of financing investment, and the prospect of profits from investment. More recently, studies of the sort I have mentioned have shown, or at least suggested, how each of these factors behaves during cyclical fluctuations in business, and what their net effect is on decisions to invest at successive stages of the business cycle.

During the course of a business expansion, for example, the costs of acquiring and installing plant and equipment rise, and so do interest rates. To judge from investment commitments, however, profit expectations seem to rise even more rapidly and the expected rate of return to become more and more optimistic. In the late stages of expansion, however, a change takes place in this relation. Costs of plant and equipment continue to rise, it is true, and may even accelerate, and capital funds become more difficult to get at "reasonable" rates of interest. But profit prospects no longer rise more rapidly than construction and equipment and finance costs. The expected rate of return tends to flatten out and then decline, and a powerful brake is applied to plans to expand or even replace capacity.

Expectations of profits need not become dimmer to make the expected rate of return fall. But in fact, they do. What is involved, of course, is a cost-price squeeze, coupled with retardation in the rate of growth of output.

Consider the cost side of the profit margin. Labor productivity, which generally rises throughout the expansion, tends to rise less rapidly as employment becomes fuller. Wage rates, on the other hand, tend to rise more rapidly. Unit labor costs, then, tend to go up. Similar developments raise other costs. Stand-by equipment, brought back into production to meet orders that could not otherwise be filled, tend to raise the costs of fuel, labor, and the other items used in running the equipment. Steady supplies of materials become harder to get in the larger quantities required and their quality tends to deteriorate. Wastage and the proportion of "seconds" increase. Management is stretched beyond the point of optimum efficiency. As a consequence of these various developments, unit costs are pushed up.

In an increasing number of industries, however, prices cannot be raised, or raised sufficiently to offset the effects of higher unit costs. Regulations or custom may keep prices rigid, or prices may be kept down because competing products are benefiting from rapid technological advance, or because demand is no longer buoyant and may even be declining in an increasing proportion of industries, or because new capacity has just been added or is in sight.

With unit costs rising and prices rising less rapidly than these costs, on the average, profit margins begin to decline, or look as if they will decline. If at the same time output rises at a slower rate than before, as in fact often happens at this stage of the cycle, even aggregate profits may stop rising, or look as if they will. But the value of capital assets continues to expand as construction is completed and equipment delivered. The net upshot, as I have said, may be an actual or threatened decline in the average rate of return. Incentives to maintain, let alone expand, the high level of investment commitments are weakened.

These developments are clues to the future course of an important class of expenditures and therefore need to be taken into account in any economic forecast. Yet many economists making their forecasts late last year, or even earlier this year, failed to recognize, or give sufficient weight to, these signs of the emergence of restraints on business investment.

Current Developments

It may be worth taking the time to be specific. Last December the statistics suggested that output per man-hour in nonagricultural industries had stopped rising, and might even have fallen a bit since the first quarter of 1966. Wage rates and other labor costs were rising and could be expected to continue rising more rapidly than in earlier months. It was fair to conclude that unit labor costs, which had been remarkably stable for over four years, were no longer going to remain low. Industrial raw material prices had been falling, but they were still on a fairly high level, and the costs of semi-processed materials and manufactured components were probably still rising. Construction costs were high. Most firms were reporting delays in getting deliveries. The cost of financing investment was extraordinarily high by historical standards.

These developments pointed to a rise in unit costs that might be expected to continue and perhaps accelerate. Had sales been rising vigorously, profit expectations might not have been seriously affected. But in fact retail and wholesale sales were sluggish and little if any higher than nine or 12 months earlier. Manufacturers' shipments and GNP in both real and dollar terms were also showing signs of retardation. Profits per dollar of sales were already falling, and aggregate profits had stopped rising. The liabilities of business failures were up.

It was not surprising, therefore, to come upon evidence that plans to invest were weakening. Orders for machinery and equipment and contracts for commercial and industrial buildings had been sagging for some months. New capital appropriations by manufacturing companies were down from their peak in the second quarter of 1966. Housing permits and starts had been falling drastically for a year or more. In addition, the index of net business formation was down. The McGraw-Hill survey indicated that plans to spend on new plant and equipment in 1967 were only about 5 percent more than in 1966, a rise in expenditures very little different from the probable rise in prices. This meant that a decline was expected in investment volume from the highest level already reached in 1966. In a word, commitments to invest in fixed capital were already showing signs of weakness in the last quarter of 1966, and what could then be seen of the factors that determine these commitments did not justify hope that recovery would soon come in that area.

The inadequate attention paid to these developments may well have accounted for the optimism about 1967 expressed by many forecasters at the time. One may wonder whether this is not also the situation today, and I'll have a word to say about that in a moment.

Information for Forecasting

Because too many people think of economic forecasting as a mysterious process involving supernatural if not divine inspiration, I have been insisting on the existence of a scientific basis for the forecasting. And I have even been saying that forecasting could be better than it is if more use were made of the available knowledge. Yet even at its best, the knowledge needed to make good forecasts is severely limited. These limitations need to be stressed, and we must underscore also the restrictions they impose on what can be said in a forecast and on the confidence with which forecasts can be held.

We would see the limitations most clearly if we were to ask what equations are required for the model, that is, explicitly or implicitly, to be used to make a numerical forecast of the gross national product (GNP), and what information goes into each of the equations. I do not intend to summarize the big book that Professor Duesenberry and his associates put together on the Brookings quarterly model a couple of years ago. It *is* a big book, containing a system of equations that number more than 150. But if one wants an idea of what information is needed, a glance at it would be illuminating.

Let me merely say—I am simplifying drastically—that one needs to estimate the direct and indirect consequences for the future of each major class of expenditures—consumption, investment, government, and net exports—of what has already happened and of what may be expected to happen. We do know a good deal about the factors affecting investment and what has been happening to them, for example, but it is doubtful that we know enough to make, with anything like precision, the numerical estimates that are required. The surveys I have mentioned provide useful information on businessmen's expectations of investment outlays, but expectations may be disappointed. The surveys therefore constitute only one of the items of information to be used in formulating a forecast of investment. And our knowledge of the contribution of each of these items of information—or of the weights to be assigned to them—is rather uncertain. In technical language, the investment function we have is still very primitive. Also, to make a forecast of GNP requires taking account not only of governmental actions already in being or clearly in prospect, but of those that will be induced by what happens—or even by the forecasts of what might happen. And this requires knowing, or guessing, not what governmental authorities say they will do but what they will do. And there are, of course, the difficulties of determining the effects of other "special" or "exogenous" factors. Whether the war will heat up or cool down is usually handled by an explicit assumption, but there are other special factors, less potentially important but not unimportant, the appearance and quantitative effects of which must somehow be estimated or ignored or assumed away.

Uncertainty and Forecasting

I do not want to turn this meeting into a forecasting session, but I should at least illustrate more specifically how some of the difficulties of forecasting make for uncertainties about the outlook. Let us consider the economic situation today.

You will recall my description of the situation as it appeared in December. Since the turn of the year, about three months of information has been added. According to the latest figures, (mostly for February or March, as I have mentioned) unit labor costs in manufacturing industries have risen again and are now about 5 percent above a year ago, and there is no reason to expect payroll costs to rise less rapidly in 1967 than in 1966. Industrial material prices have fallen further, but wholesale prices excluding farm products and foods have risen further. Construction costs are also higher. While interest rates have fallen, they are still high. Profit margins are down still more. With industrial output down, it is likely that aggregate profits in the first quarter will probably also be down. The liabilities of failures and the number of large business failures have increased. The physical volume of retail sales still seems sluggish, despite the jump between February and March, and the prospects of a strong export demand are not good. Constant-price GNP in the first quarter of 1967 is estimated as no higher than in the last quarter of 1966. Contracts and orders for plant and equipment have fallen further. Plans to put up housing have shown signs of revival, but their level is still very low. Business formation is a bit below the level of three months ago. The McGraw-Hill survey of investment plans has been revised upward a trifle. But the Commerce-

SEC survey of expected expenditures on plant and equipment, conducted in late January and February, indicates a rise of only 4 percent between 1966 and 1967. This means that bare maintenance of the fourth quarter 1966 level is expected—and if account is taken of probable price increases, an actual decline in investment volume is anticipated.

The easier monetary policy and the probable restoration of the investment credit may be expected to strengthen investment demand. Housing construction will follow the rise in permits and starts. But this may take some time. The rate of inventory investment has fallen sharply, but with sales still sluggish, it is possible for inventory investment to fall still further and remain negative for a while.

For some months, then, perhaps extending into the fall or even beyond, investment demand can continue weak and even become weaker. This possibility certainly should not be excluded from the range of what seems relevant as one looks ahead, even though no one can express the expected level of investment in anything like a precise quantity.

A further weakening of investment demand and then expenditures could lead to a further reduction in industrial output and construction activity. If this should happen, we could hardly expect employment and payrolls in industry and then also in other branches of the private economy, to remain untouched. And these reductions could, in turn, cause declines in consumption. The so-called built-in stabilizers can be expected to slow down such a cumulation of forces making for recession, but they cannot be expected to stop them.

On the other hand, the economy could start to move up vigorously after the middle of the year, once inventories are in line, and business fixed investment has come down to but not fallen below a "sustainable rate."

What I am getting at is this: At the present time, no one can be sure what the economy will do during the rest of the year. No one, in other words, knows how much stimulus will result from the easing of monetary policy, the release of frozen federal funds, the restoration of the investment credit, and the other actions that are in sight or have already been taken to encourage business. No one can be sure these will do as much as is needed and do it quickly enough to prevent a recession if one is actually in the making. If I am right, neither of the two possibilities I have mentioned can be said to outweigh the other so heavily as to make it unnecessary to give serious attention to both.

If forecasts are to take account also of possible courses of governmental action induced by the unfolding of events, including developments abroad—as the forecasts should—the number of possible futures that need to be considered becomes greater. No private economist can be sure what government will do or what will be the effects of what it does. But the problem confronts also the government economist. One gets the impression that the fiscal authorities are not always sure what the monetary authorities will do and vice versa. Nor can the executive branch be sure what the legislative branch will agree to, nor what the executive branch will want or need to do as circumstances change.

Limitations on Forecasters' Knowledge

The limitations on the knowledge of forecasters have important implications for what can be claimed for forecasting. Too much is claimed by a forecaster, it seems to me, when he comes out with *a* forecast of GNP in the year ahead; when his forecast is expressed in terms of a definite figure—even if it is identified as being at the middle of a range, and even if the range is specified in some way; and when his estimate for the year is distributed over the two halves or four quarters of the year.

The scientific basis of forecasting is such that the case is stronger for indicating the several more likely possibilities than for concentrating on one only; for saying something about the direction of movement, than for stating the amount of change; for saying something about the pressure being built up for a change in direction, than for specifying the date for a change in direction.

To avoid misunderstanding, perhaps I should mention that I do not suppose it would be helpful or even feasible to try to specify *every* possible eventuality. But surely the major—the more probable—futures need to be mentioned. When, as is usually the case, only one forecast is offered, it should be made clear that the forecaster has made up his own mind about the policies that will be followed and their consequences, and also about the other major special factors that will influence events. And what he has assumed should be specified.

If forecasts had no influence on the policy decisions of government and of private citizens, it would not matter what was put into them and what precision was claimed for them. But they do influence these decisions to a significant degree. Forecasts would be more useful or less dangerous if their limitations were admitted and no more were put into them and no more certainty claimed for them than is reasonable in the light of tested knowledge. Perhaps single-valued, unconditional forecasts are made because businessmen and government officials ask for forecasts free of "ifs, ands, and buts." If so, this demand should be resisted. The caveat appended to a forecast of GNP—that it is subject to uncertainty—does not convey a proper sense of the uncertainties if a single estimate is given and it is expressed in units as small as a billion dollars. We live in an uncertain world. It is better to recognize this. And if we do, we will be more alert to change, and quicker to make use of the information that comes into view to revise our forecasts and adjust our policies.

Appraising the Accuracy of Forecasts

The uncertainties surrounding economic forecasting are emphasized by an appraisal by the National Bureau of a sample of short-term forecasts made by a variety of individuals and agencies over the period between 1953-63. The report, by Professor Victor Zarnowitz, appeared only a few weeks ago, and you may not have yet had a chance to digest it. The conclusions of the study that are especially interesting for our present purposes are, first, that forecasts of GNP for the year ahead, or for the next one to three quarters, did better, on the average, than simple mechanical extrapolations of past rates of change. Second, while the mean absolute error of the forecasts for the calendar year ahead (about $10 billion) was no more than 2 percent of the average level of GNP in the period 1953-63, it was about 40 percent of the average year-to-year change in GNP—and it is the latter that constitutes the primary objective of short-term forecasting. Third, the accuracy of the forecasts analyzed diminished as the forecast span increased. The forecasts for four quarters or more ahead were generally not superior to simple extrapolations of the recent average rate of change. Nor, fourth, were the multi-period forecasts able to predict turning points in aggregate output ahead of the turn.

Another National Bureau study by Professor Rendigs Fels covers forecasts published over the period 1948-61. It is described in the annual report of the Bureau, for 1966-67. Fels confirms the findings by Zarnowitz that few forecasts succeed in forecasting cyclical peaks and troughs, and adds that few forecasters were very successful even in quickly recognizing cyclical peaks when they had already occurred. It is only fair to add that because of the lag in current information, forecasts must "in effect predict a little backward in time as well as forward," as Zarnowitz points out.

Forecasting and Government Policies

It is not always easy to decide whether a forecast has been right. Suppose the forecast simply specifies what may be expected if government takes no action to alter the course of events. If the forecast leads to action by government, what happens will differ from what was forecast.

Perhaps the "rolling adjustment" of 1962 provides an example. The narrowing of the scope of the expansion, and the declines in the stock market, in orders for machinery and equipment, and in other leading indicators during the spring —a tendency which the "steel affair" in April may well have reinforced—led economists advising the new administration to set the probability of trouble ahead at an uncomfortably high level. By mid-1962, according to Theodore Sorenson, they were pointing to "the developing recession." But they also argued for a tax cut. While the tax cut did not in fact come until many months later, official talk of it began soon and public confidence that it would come was stimulated. Along with the liberalization of depreciation accounting for tax purposes, the passage of the investment credit, and the steps taken to reassure businessmen that direct price and profit controls were not in the cards, it might well have served to nip the incipient recession in the bud. After some hesitation—and before developments had reached the stage at which a recession could be recorded—the business expansion had resumed its course.

What has been happening in recent months could conceivably turn out to provide another example. The stage of the business cycle is quite different now, of course, and we have to make the best of the mistakes of 1965 and 1966. We should therefore expect—if a recession were in fact avoided—that there would be more rapid price increase and less rapid output increase than in 1962-65.

It goes without saying that we will never have all the information we want. But I think we can make substantial improvements if we try. And we can learn to organize this information better. A few brief observations must suffice to indicate what I have in mind.

First, it is desirable to improve the current flow of information. One of the reasons why the long expansion that began in 1961 developed the symptoms it did in 1966 is because adequate information on the size of the military buildup in 1965 was not available. Had the information been available, it would have been easier to see the inflationary pressures accumulating; and the price and cost developments that became visible in 1966 might have been anticipated. A tax increase or a tightening of monetary policy would have been politically difficult, even with the information available. But its absence made the danger more difficult to recognize and reduced the chances of corrective action to a negligible level. What was needed, and what is still needed, is better and prompter information on the vastly important area of government commitments and expenditures. A reasonably detailed quarterly federal budget, prepared on the several bases now conventional, with projections revised to take account of major changes, would not be easy to prepare. As many economists have been saying, however, it would be worth the trouble.

Second, existing information can be better mobilized. There are grounds for suspecting that the country is more sensitive to the dangers of recession than to the dangers of inflation, for example. An insensitivity to inflationary pressures can lead to the neglect of developments that threaten serious problems for the future. One way to heighten the country's sensitivity to inflation would be to put together a set of "indicators of inflation" and bring it to the attention of the public on occasion or even regularly. Much of the material is already at hand in *Business Cycle Developments* and other government publications. But there are gaps that need to be filled in, especially on wages and other payroll costs. Publication of such information would make it more difficult to ignore a buildup of inflationary pressures.

Third, much needs to be done to improve and deepen understanding of measurements that are widely used in assessing the economic situation—the rate of unemployment, the balance-of-payments deficit, the federal budgetary deficit, GNP, and wages including fringe benefits. The rate of unemployment, for example, is a key indicator to which much attention is rightly paid. Yet this indicator has been changing in meaning and significance over the years. In a study currently underway at the National Bureau, also described in the annual report, Professor Jacob Mincer points to the increase that has taken place in the proportion of "peripheral" workers in the labor force. These persons, married women, retirement-age adults, and school-age youths, tend to move in and out of the labor force according to economic conditions. Their mobility causes them to experience a relatively high rate of transitional unemployment. During an upswing, then, when the expansion is reducing the incidence and duration of unemployment of the "regular" members of the labor force, it is at the same time attracting into the labor force persons who will be looking for jobs. Beyond a certain point, an expansion in aggregate demand may fail to reduce the overall unemployment rate. This has obvious implications for the significance of short- and long-term changes in unemployment and for the guidance of economic policy.

Improving Economic Forecasts

Finally, much more needs to be done to improve methods of forecasting. What forecasters now depend upon is essentially a mixture of chart reading and paper and pencil calculations blended with elements of hunch through an exercise of judgment. What is needed is a practical forecasting procedure that makes use of all the relevant information, organizes this information in a systematic and explicit way that can be followed, and extracts from the information an internally consistent forecast accompanied by a specification of its probable error.

The econometric models to which I referred a few moments ago offer the best promise of eventually providing such a procedure. They are not, in principle, different from the less systematic approaches, since all approaches make or can make use of the same information, and have to deal with the same problems—the problem of interaction among the various elements of the economic system and the problem of estimating the effects of exogenous factors. The so-called indicators approach —when it is not merely mechanical chart reading—uses Mitchell's business cycle theory, which can be translated into a model or system of equations, as Friedman once indicated. The so-called GNP approach by many business economists also in effect uses a model and solves the problem of interaction with an iterative process of approximation rather than by the solution of simultaneous equations. But the approaches do differ in the way in which they organize and use the information, and in the amounts, precision, and formal consistency of the information they aim to provide.

The advantage of the formal econometric model approach is that, being more explicit in the steps taken to make a forecast, it lends itself to improvement more readily than the other approaches. And one way to improve it, I might mention, is to expand it to take more account of the cost-price aspect of economic change than it now does.

At the present time, the econometric model is still in the experimental stage and far from the practical instrument it may become. Its chief defect arises precisely out of the fact that the econometric model, being so explicit and orderly and apparently complete, seems to require less hunch and judgment than the less systematic procedures that are widely followed. When better information becomes available, and in fact less hunch and judgment are required, the comparative advantage of the econometric model will grow and it may eventually displace or absorb the other approaches.

Even when the art or science of forecasting has reached the point at which a single, comprehensive approach is generally used, however, we may expect differences in the results. For whatever the approach, to make an economic forecast requires that estimates be made of the likelihood of various prospective developments abroad as well as in this country, in the political as well as the economic sphere, and also in technology, the weather, and so on. On these, judgments by economists as well as others are bound to vary. But improvements in forecasting should help to narrow the differences among forecasts.

I have said enough, I think, to elicit discussion. Let me add only that the present state of forecasting—the fact that forecasting is neither utterly useless nor really very good—has important implications for policy. The basic question, of course, is that of rules versus authorities. Because forecasting is not very good, we cannot afford to spurn the assistance of general rules or principles as a basis of policy. And this being the case, it would be wise to devote more attention to improving these rules. It would be well also to strengthen our automatic stabilizers.

But we cannot depend on rules and automatic devices only. We are bound to react to what we can see coming, even if we can see it only dimly. This requires flexible policy administered by authorities and, of course, better information to guide them.

Wiser rules, improved automatic stabilizers, and more competent and better informed authorities will not serve to eliminate all cyclical fluctuations in employment and output, however. I do not believe we want to try to do so, since we do not want to sacrifice other national goals to attain complete stability. We must therefore take steps also to do more than we now do for those of our citizens who bear the brunt of a decline in economic activity.

DISCUSSION AND COMMENTS ON PAPERS BY PROFESSOR McCRACKEN AND PROFESSOR FABRICANT

Professor Henry C. Wallich

I would like to reverse the order of the papers and turn first to Dr. Fabricant. One cannot but be impressed by the scholarly restraint which Sol Fabricant imposes upon forecasts and we all ought to take this very much to heart. The trouble is that the need for forecasts is strong.

The need for forecasts in government rises from several sources, one of them is the budget, another is the fact that our policies function with a lag. If a change in monetary and fiscal policy takes six months to achieve a good part of its effect, then it is useless to look at the present without having some idea of the future.

The condition in which the economy actually finds itself shows how very difficult that is. We don't even know the present, let alone the future. We don't know if we are in a recession or not.

Dr. Fabricant, therefore, is amply borne out by our present situation. Nevertheless, when I see the constraints he wants to impose on a forecaster, I wonder how much useful forecasting we will have.

First, he says, it is bad to give one single GNP number,

better give several. Second, it is safer not to name a number but to indicate the direction in which the GNP is likely to move, and, third safer still, not to give the time when this move will come but talk about the pressures that are building up for a move, if and when.

Here is a conflict between the detached scientists and the operating, not to say political, economists. We are condemned to forecast. If we immure ourselves in a high ivory tower, we can say to ourselves, I would rather be right than be chairman of the Council of Economic Advisers. But we will be superseded and somebody else will be doing the forecasting. It isn't that we can prevent bad forecasts from being made; we just make sure that others will make them. Here is the difficulty I see with Professor Fabricant's proposal.

Now, turning to Paul McCracken, I think Paul's excellent paper said many things that needed saying. He pointed to the relative historical stability of the economy. He pointed out that the 1960s have not been all that extraordinary. He raised some very important questions about fine tuning of the economy which apparently also is a great concern to Mr. Mills.

I do have some questions, and I am sure that these are not in the least new to Paul, about his interpretation of the data.

We look at cycles back to the nineteenth century. I can never convince myself that the nineteenth century is very relevant to what goes on today. If you look at any particular market, either the money market or the steel market, if there is some old-timer who tells you how it was done in 1890, I don't think anybody is guided by that. We had flexible prices in those days, for one thing. I hesitate to rely on Paul's evidence of past stability.

I hesitate to rely on stable relationships of the economy to money. Paul has one stable relationship in his paper which he largely left out in his oral presentation. I, therefore, have to throw away some other money relationships that I computed which show just the opposite. It all depends on how you define money, including time deposits or excluding them. If you include time deposits, why not give the savings and loans a break? These ratios all behave differently.

Where we come to the real core of the problem is in drawing the conclusion that the government ought to do much less and ought to proceed much more stably. This is, I think, a currently—I hate to use the word—fashionable conclusion, but it is a conclusion that a great many people are now drawing from the recent performance or misperformance of the economy. To some extent, it is attributable to mishandling—to overstabilization, both on the part of the government and, to some extent, by the Federal Reserve.

Does it follow from this that we ought to set these data on a kind of automatic pilot, raise the money supply at a constant rate, set the budgets so that full employment will produce a small surplus or will produce balance, and then let events take their course? I think I probably exaggerate a little what Paul McCracken had in mind. But there are others who more or less suggest this. Set the dials and then don't fiddle with them.

One problem here again is that the dials are not unambiguous. As I said a minute ago, money ratios to GNP depend on what kind of a definition of money you choose. The full-employment surplus is another wobbly number, as Paul knows very well. The effect of a budget depends not only on the full-employment surplus but also on the absolute magnitude of the budget, because of a balanced budget multiplier. A budget that is balanced, say, at $150 billion for expenditures and revenues is not the same in its economic impact as a budget which is balanced at $160 billion. If you move from $150 to $160 billion by raising expenditures and revenues, you ought to raise revenues more in order to prevent that budget from becoming expansionary.

This is one defect that I see in the fixed dial settings. The other is again practical and, if I may, I invite you to visualize Paul McCracken now as chairman of the Council of Economic Advisers and, if somebody would want to construe this as a forecast, I will not quarrel with him, then the conversation might go something like this:

The President says, "Paul, it looks as though we are in a bad recession, what can we do?" Paul says, "Mr. President, we have set the rate of growth of the money supply at 4 percent. We expect the budget to produce a balance at full employment, so we can't tamper with this now."

You know exactly what would happen. The political pressures would compel the President to break the rules. He would get the Fed to ease more rapidly, if they can. He would certainly do something to increase expenditures. He would possibly propose a tax cut. As soon as a crisis is upon us of any sort, we are going to break the rules, therefore, I don't think it wise to establish rules in the first place.

Furthermore, if we compare the behavior of the economy with rules and without, we are always giving the rules the break because we never have to suffer the consequence of the trouble the rules would have gotten us into, had they been followed. What kind of a mess might we have been in had we been on a 4 percent money growth rule in 1960 with the tremendous payments deficit, when money was going out in large amounts? We might have been knocked off the dollar peg. According to Milton Friedman that might not have been bad; he argues we ought to have flexible rates as a complement to a stable money growth rule.

I have said enough here. I would dearly like to see us do better in fiscal policy. I do not think that going in the direction of stabler rules is the way.

Professor Arthur Smithies

I'm glad, after listening to Henry Wallich, to see that at least one man can survive employment by the United States government and emerge from it with his sense of humor unimpaired.

I feel our main speakers, on the contrary, have been somewhat too apologetic. Paul McCracken had harsh words for the recession of 1958, which he participated in creating. And Sol Fabricant has been engaged in an eminent institution for most of his life that has engaged in economic forecasting and I feel he has beaten his breast a bit too much in public, and I was rather concerned about him committing himself to the econometric model in the last part of his paper. Despite what Milton Friedman has done to Wesley Mitchell, I still draw a sharp distinction between the National Bureau approach and the econometric model-building approach. I find them both useful, and I would like to see the National Bureau, even if it's old-fashioned and perhaps overly respectable, continue on its present general course.

Like Henry, I have been struck by the flirtation that both our papers have had with automatic rules but I feel neither of the main authors has been completely seduced. I have felt attracted by these devices in the past and I think I share their present position.

One point about the full employment budget, before I forget it. Paul McCracken regarded this as a new discovery of recent years. I would like to remind him, in the interest of his historical researches, that this idea, like most ideas is not a new one. As far as I know, it was due to Beardsley Ruml in the early forties and it has been consistently put forward by the Committee for Economic Development. It is only recently that it has penetrated official statements and publications, which is a very good thing.

The further point about forecasting which I would like to emphasize, which Sol mentions, is that forecasters are, to some extent, misjudged in public because forecasts do tend either to be self-fulfilling or self-defeating, and when you compare the actual record of the forecast, one has to take that into account. The influential forecaster is like a fortune-teller or like the Oracle of Delphi, if you go back to classical times with Henry, and people act, to some extent, on the basis of the forecast. If the fortune-teller tells someone he is going to meet a beautiful girl on the street, the man may go out of the fortune-teller's office, look over all of the girls on the street and believe he has found a beautiful one as a result of the fortune-telling.

On the other hand, the policeman may be warned that the fortune-teller is going to tell people that there is going to be a beautiful girl on the street and the policeman may come around and stop him finding one. This sort of thing happens in government. Forecasts tend to be self-fulfilling, as far as the bulk of the private economy is concerned. But forecasts may be self-defeating, to the extent that they induce the authorities to prevent them from coming true. As Sol has also pointed out, the pessimistic forecasts at the beginning of this year may have helped to bring prompt action on the part of the Federal Reserve Board.

Also, if I can go back to history, I participated in some of the forecasts of depression at the end of World War II. I think these forecasts themselves forced the government into kinds of action that may of itself have helped to avert a postwar recession.

Now, I want to turn to Paul McCracken's highly interesting paper, particularly to his assertion that most of the instability in recorded history has come from the actions of government. Obviously, there is something to be said for this but I think in fairness to government it is important to consider the type of action that tends to produce the instability because it is not always mistaken fiscal policy. There are four possibilities which may lead to destabilizing government action.

First is the impact of external events, particularly wars. I think you can trace most of the instability that he is talking about to wars or their aftermath and contrary to the impression that is sometimes given in the contemporary press, I don't believe that wars are engaged in for the sake of fiscal policy or because national administrations like them. I can't imagine any administration liking anything less than a war and they have to adapt themselves as best they can. So this kind of instability can't be credited to incompetence of government in the economic field, at any rate.

Secondly, some instabilities can and do arise from serious mistakes in diagnosis and prescription and the famous episode of the Federal Reserve in 1933 is, of course, a case in point.

For the sake of that admirable institution, and for the sake of the future I wish this episode could be forgotten. It is like holding a college grade of E against someone for the rest of his career. Surely the Federal Reserve would not make that kind of a mistake again. Like the rest of us, it can learn from experience.

A third point is that government policy, as I think we all know, is not entirely the product of the economists or financial advisers to the government. Economic policy very frequently is a matter of politics and it's hard to think of any economic policy that is not largely affected by political attitudes and pressures. It is tremendously hard, for instance, for the authorities to control a boom. Everyone loves a boom. Profits go up. Revenues go up. Wages go up. Everything goes up and the spoilsport stabilizer has an awfully hard time trying to stop it.

Another point is that there is a continual conflict in our society between those who fear inflation more than those who fear unemployment. Both inflation and unemployment are legitimate fears and serious social evils. How you weigh the one danger against the other is very largely a matter of political values. I think a lot of the vicissitudes in our economic policy come from honest and sincere differences in attitude between and among people concerning those two social evils.

My fourth point about government is there is some need for the government to act in a destabilizing way from the point of view of the performance of the overall economy. Unfortunately we have not got any method, any adequate method for controlling wages and prices that is consistent with a smoothly running fiscal and monetary policy. Everyone shudders at the idea of compulsory controls of the wartime variety, and experience has clearly shown that these controls are inhibiting in the long run and will only last for a short period in any case.

So the wage-price question is one of the great unsolved problems of our society and the only thing we are left with are the old fiscal and monetary weapons. If wages and prices go too far and the balance of payments gets out of gear, then the authorities have to put on the brakes. That looks destabilizing from the point of view of the internal operation of the economy.

So government, I think, shouldn't be blamed for some of these destabilizations. I now come back to 1958. I don't think that the nature of the action that was taken in 1958 was wrong but the magnitude of it was wrong. The authorities moved in the right direction. I have always had more sympathy for that episode than many of the critics of it have had.

Now, two remarks about the present situation. Both of our speakers have criticized the government for not producing reliable estimates of war expenditures. To some extent, I agree with this criticism. I think the Defense Department could have done much better. But I would like to remind you that this war is a different kind of war from any that we have been engaged in before. We are trying to fight this novel kind of thing called a limited war where the war is not being fought to some specified military conclusion. In contrast, in the second World War, the aim was unconditional surrender. In the Korean War, the aim was not only to defeat the military enemy but to reconstitute the entire defense structure of the country, and it was perfectly clear, to those of us who were concerned with policies in the Korean War what ought to be done.

At the present time, I think it would be contrary to the idea of a limited war for the government to be able to produce precise estimates of military expenditures for the next two years, because that's not its objective. It is trying to stop the war instead of trying to continue it. So I think the government ought to be treated with some sympathy on that point.

And the last point I want to make again comes back to the Federal Reserve Board and the Federal Reserve System. For some of these political reasons that I was referring to earlier I think fiscal policy has been unavailable. I think most economists would have recommended a tax increase in 1965. For a variety of reasons, we didn't do that. One of the reasons was that the 1964 tax cut was pronounced as permanent and eternal. It seems to me at that time we should have said that circumstances might occur where taxes ought to go up again, and we didn't say that.

But the facts of the matter are that the Federal Reserve System has been left as the only stabilizer in the country. It has been supposed to maintain stability of employment and stability of prices at the same time with one major instrument in its control, and it is an axiom of economics that you have to have as many instruments of policy as you do have objectives of policy. I personally feel that the Federal Reserve System has done well under the circumstances that were forced upon it.

In conclusion, I don't feel the pessimism that our papers to some extent seem to exhibit. My counsel is usually less than perfection, our policies have been less than perfect, but I don't think they have been too bad.

Mr. Robert W. Stone

Dr. McCracken analyzes the performance record of fiscal policy in terms of the behavior of the full-employment budget, and the record of monetary policy in terms of changes in the rate of monetary expansion. I have no quarrel with his analysis of the record of fiscal policy. But I am troubled by his appraisal of monetary policy. More specifically, since his appraisal rests on his particular definition of what constitutes a change in monetary policy, I am troubled by his definition. In seeking an unambiguous way of expressing the meaning of the terms monetary ease or tightness, he says, "a more rapid rate of monetary expansion is an easier monetary policy than a slower expansion."

Now those who are not closely engaged in following these matters might infer that the Federal Reserve uses the money supply as its policy target—that when it decides to change policy, it decides to change the rate of monetary expansion and then proceeds to do so. But this is not so. The Fed does not proceed in this way. Indeed, while Dr. McCracken's formulation suggests that GNP follows the path set out by the rate of monetary expansion, my own conception of the matter, based on the way in which monetary policy is actually executed, suggests that in good part it is the other way around; that is, that a good part of the time, although not always, the rate of monetary expansion follows the path of GNP, which, in turn, is responding to a wide variety of influences.

This, I am aware, is not a popular view with a great many economists. On the other hand, it is one of the contested issues in current economics and I'd like briefly to join the debate. I do so here not because we are concerned with monetary policy per se but because I think the way in which the problem of monetary policy is viewed can condition in a significant way the kind of fiscal policy one would regard as appropriate in given circumstances. Thus I think there is ample room in this session on fiscal policy for some focusing on the closely related question of monetary policy.

I have already noted that Dr. McCracken defines changes in monetary policy in terms of changes in the rate of monetary expansion. If we can agree on what is meant by the term "monetary expansion" I would have to concede that his definition has the virtue of clarity, but the difficulty, in my view is, that that definition is not very helpful, for it is not descriptive of the actual process by which changes in monetary policy are made. And so I will venture my own definition. I would say that a change in monetary policy occurs when the Federal Reserve changes the terms on which it is prepared to provide the banking system with additional reserves.

Now I hasten to note that this definition obviously lacks the virtues of clarity and precision. But at the same time it does have the merit of being descriptive of the actual process by which the Fed undertakes what I conceive to be a change in policy.

Let me illustrate. Monetary policy or, more specifically, open-market policy, which is my major concern here, is executed at the trading desk of the New York Fed under the direction of the Manager of the Open Market Account.

The Manager's instructions from the Open Market Committee, which formulates the policy and which meets every three or four weeks, run in terms of money market conditions. The operative part of a typical directive from the Committee to the Manager might read, "System open-market operations during the next three weeks shall be conducted with a view to maintaining about the same conditions in the money market as have prevailed in recent weeks." This is the kind of directive the Manager gets and this is what he must go by. But what does it mean?

The money market reflects the rate at which money is being demanded in relation to the existing supply of it. If additional amounts of money are being demanded at a given rate as GNP grows, for example, those additional demands will be reflected in the money market by a tendency for interest rates to rise; and there would be a corollary tendency for banks' required reserves to rise and for net free reserves to fall.

In those circumstances, the Manager, with his instructions to "maintain about the same money market conditions as have recently prevailed," would put additional reserves into the market and, on the basis of those additional reserves, there would occur a multiple expansion of bank credit and deposits to meet the additional demands for money that were reflected in the market and to which the manager responded. Thus interest rates would not rise; money market conditions would remain unchanged. The demands for additional amounts of money would have been met on the same terms as in the recent past.

Let us suppose, owing perhaps to a vigorous dose of fiscal stimulation or to some other influence, the rate at which additional amounts of money is demanded increases. Here the upward pressure on interest rates would be intensified; and if the Manager had the same instructions we used a moment ago, he would have to provide reserves at a faster rate than formerly in order to "maintain about the same conditions in the money market." That faster rate of reserve expansion would, in such circumstances, be reflected in a faster rate of monetary expansion. By the time of the next meeting of the Open Market Committee, this faster rate of monetary expansion (and perhaps other indications of gathering steam) might be reflected in the figures then available. The Committee might then instruct the Manager to maintain firmer money market conditions over the next few weeks than prevailed over the last few. If the Committee so instructs the Manager, it would, to go back to my rough-and-ready definition, have changed policy in the sense that it would have changed the terms on which it is prepared to provide additional reserves. The Manager would not supply any reserves at the interest rate levels at which he supplied them in the preceding period; he would supply them only at higher interest rate levels. If, despite those higher rate levels, reserves were still demanded and supplied at what the Fed regarded as too rapid a rate, it might at the next meeting give the Manager a new instruction to maintain still firmer money market conditions in the ensuing period.

The foregoing brief sketch of the actual process by which policy is executed has been designed to illustrate the underlying point that, within any three or four week policy period, and setting aside the current experiment with the so-called bank credit proxy, the Fed so conducts its policy that reserves are on tap; the Fed's posture is accommodative; in textbook language, its supply schedule for reserves is horizontal. Thus the volume of reserves that will actually be provided depends upon the volume that will be demanded on the terms the Fed specifies; and the volume demanded depends largely on the demand for money, which, in turn, is closely related to GNP. The initiative rests with the demand side and not with the supply side. Thus, while Dr. McCracken says that, "the economy is not apt to stray far from the trail being blazed by the pace of monetary expansion," I think it might be as fair to say that monetary expansion is not apt to stray far from the trail being blazed by the economy.

This is obviously not to assert that monetary policy has little or nothing to do with what happens to the economy. Under the impact of policy, as I conceive it to be actually conducted, money can become so expensive and, for any individual borrower, so difficult to obtain as to frustrate and abort spending plans. And, on the other hand, it can become so cheap and so readily available that it can trigger decisions to spend or to add to cash balances. When the former happens, the rate of monetary expansion will slow, as it did last summer; and when the latter happens, it will rise, as it has done recently. I am thus suggesting that the rate of growth of GNP is partly dependent on the terms on which the Fed is prepared to supply reserves and that the rate of monetary expansion is a function of the rate at which reserves are demanded on those terms.

Let me now, after this discussion of monetary policy, come back to a point I made earlier. That is, the choice among alternative approaches to monetary policy can greatly condition the kind of fiscal policy that is likely to be employed under given circumstances. Dr. McCracken would have monetary policy trace out a path of reasonably steady monetary expansion. Since GNP is subject to a great many influences other than the rate of monetary expansion, we could experience, under such an approach, wide swings in interest rates as the steady rate of monetary expansion at times flooded the economy with liquidity and at other times aborted attempts of the economy to grow faster. However steady our economic growth might be in aggregative terms, we might well be subjected to serious distortions and imbalances in certain economic sectors. The high level of interest rates necessary to frustrate an attempt to grow faster could put a substantial squeeze on such a sector as housing, which depends upon a good flow of funds through intermediaries specializing in the financing of that sector. Or, on the other side, the low level of interest rates associated with a reduced demand for money—which could occur despite the steady rate at which it is being supplied—could have seriously damaging effects on the external sector.

Would there be a policy response to such sector imbalances? Quite possibly there would be. If it were to be a general and not a selective response (which in a reasonably free economy we would wish to minimize), then the response would presumably come largely from the fiscal side, since monetary policy, which would have been assigned the major role in keeping the overall economy on course, would proceed along its steady path. But could fiscal policy respond with the requisite swiftness and flexibility? I doubt it. I suspect that, as has happened in the past, fiscal policy might well undergo a heavy lurch in what seems at the same time to be the right direction, but which later turns out to have been the wrong direction. In short, I doubt that fiscal policy has reached the stage of development where it could adequately handle the tasks that would be imposed upon it by adherence to a monetary policy that called for a generally steady rate of monetary expansion.

In concluding, let me state that I agree wholeheartedly with Paul McCracken that we ought to have a substantially improved flow of budget information; that we ought to employ a better budget concept than we have in the past, and above all, I think, that we ought to try to set fiscal policy on a much steadier and less erratic course. But at the same time we ought to bear in mind that economic disturbances requiring a policy response can still arise in the private sector or from outside the system altogether. If this is so, I think the important objective of getting fiscal policy on course and keeping it there is better served by giving monetary policy free rein to make swift and flexible responses than to subject it to the constraint of achieving a generally steady rate of monetary expansion.

Professor William J. Fellner

I think, as Henry Wallich said, we are condemned to forecasting. Any purposeful human action rests on forecasts, predictions and that goes for monetary and fiscal policy as it goes for other purposeful human action. The question, really, is what kind of forecasting? What is the nature of the forecasting on which we build these policies? In this regard, various types of policy attitudes differ. As a matter of fact, the three main types of policy attitude which were distinguished in this discussion differ from one another mainly in that they involve reliance on different types of forecasting and prediction because these types of fiscal and monetary policy do not really differ from one another in ultimate objectives. They differ from one another in the kind of forecasting on which one would be basing these policies. By the three main types of monetary-fiscal policy which came up for discussion here during this session I mean the following.

First, the policy of keeping the so-called full-employment surplus reasonably stable, presumably at a moderate positive level but, at any rate, reasonably stable, and keeping the rate of increase in the money supply reasonably stable. This is a type of policy which Professor McCracken explained to us here and discussed in his paper. Another policy is that of watching turning points, trying to learn from advance indicators when we are about to experience a turning point, or trying to make a prompt diagnosis when we have experienced a turning point and making adjustments in the policy variables when these turning points have been spotted. The third type of policy that has been considered is that of placing more reliance on detailed econometric models and presumably adjusting one's policy variables to what one expects to happen in the near future on the basis of such models.

I will first say a few words about the policy of keeping the full-employment surplus reasonably stable or, if possible, quite stable, and of keeping the rate of increase of the money supply stable. Now, my reaction to this is that the positive arguments that can be made for this policy are unconvincing. But I am aware of the fact that this does not settle the question, because the other policies that are available have their weaknesses. Indeed, circumstances are conceivable in which the shortcomings of the other policies are so grave that the policy which I am considering first has advantages.

Why do I consider the positive arguments for the stable full-employment surplus and the constant rate of increase in the money supply, weak or unconvincing?

In the first place, the full-employment policy requires estimating the elasticity of various types of tax revenues with respect to output quite accurately and that kind of estimate is shaky, as indeed are the estimates of the elasticity of government expenditures, on the basis of existing programs, with respect to output. Without such an estimate as to what the tax revenue would be at capacity output, given the tax rates, and what government expenditures would be on the basis of current programs, one can't follow this policy. More importantly, the policy requires placing a definite number on the concept of "capacity output" and that would have to be a very arbitrary number. One reason is that one must make an estimate with respect to the productivity of all inputs and, by implication, technological progress. The concept of the capacity output is an arbitrary concept which involves, among other things, placing a definite number on the concept of the full employment of labor.

The full-employment estimates would be notoriously arbitrary and I would go one step beyond that and I would say that it is definitely undesirable to try to define the full employment of labor in terms of a specific percentage point of unemployment of the labor force. It is undesirable because the social consequences of any given percentage point of unemployment are very different, depending on the composition of that unemployment and on the duration of that unemployment as Professors Fabricant and Mincer have pointed out.

It is also undesirable because when economic activity rises to very high levels certain harmful developments that should be avoided will always occur, the timing of which depends on the special characteristics of each period and the level of employment and unemployment. In those circumstances, I think it is a mistake to be committed to some definite magnitude, which one calls capacity output and the full employment of labor.

In addition, I would say there are the considerations which Henry Wallich pointed out, namely, that a balanced budget at full employment means very different things, depending on what level of expenditures and taxes keep that budget balanced. This is a line of argument which, to the best of my knowledge, was first developed as the balanced-budget theorem by Professor Wallich himself in the *Quarterly Journal of Eco-*

nomics in 1944 and which he summarized in one sentence in this session.

As for keeping the rate of increase of the money supply stable, the concept of the money supply is not a very clearcut one. If you look around in the literature, you will find several definitions of the money supply. It has been used in various ways and it is not really quite clear in which sense it should be used for the policy of keeping the rate of money supply growth precisely stable.

The Federal Reserve does not, of course, directly regulate the money supply and it is incapable of doing that. It is also incapable of regulating certain economic variables which have a bearing on the money supply and that could lead to something like a stable growth rate, one however, that might involve a lot of zigzagging around a long-run growth trend. The Fed could only shoot for stability of the rate of increase in the money supply for periods of some length during which divergencies would cancel out. But it simply cannot regulate the money supply in any precise fashion because this is not one of the variables directly under its control.

Lastly, I would say that I do not find it convincing to argue that periods of greater economic stability were those in which the full-employment surplus was constant and the rate of increase in the money supply was constant and that, therefore, it is desirable to achieve the stability of those variables. If you take a period of stable growth, you will find many stable time series and to select two of these and then say that the stable characteristics of the period were attributable to their behavior is somewhat arbitrary, I would say. It is true that in many periods in which something undesirable happened, there was a sudden change in the full-employment surplus but there was also a sudden change in a number of other variables that may have accounted for it.

For example, it is quite true that from fiscal 1959 to fiscal 1960, there was a very rapid change in the so-called full-employment surplus. This was pointed out by Mr. McCracken. It also is true that the restrictive influence of fiscal policy in that period shows in many simpler data. For example, just look at the administrative budget, which in this case is probably the simplest way of forming an opinion, although it is sometimes a misleading, sometimes a very naive way of doing it.

The administrative budget position changed from a deficit of $12.5 billion to a surplus of more than $1 billion, in spite of the fact that the recession had already started. So untutored commonsense would tell one that there was a very restrictive change.

On the other hand, it is true that the other policies have very serious limitations. The policy of adjusting to turning points or the policy of trusting detailed econometric models, depends on how good one's best guess is as to the near future and that is different in different periods. The best guess concerning the outcome is never an exceedingly good guess. It is sometimes a better guess and sometimes a worse guess because we have more indications or fewer indications, and it depends on how serious the consequences are of deviations from that best guess.

In certain circumstances, these flexible policies are even more dangerous than a policy of fixed rules which Mr. McCracken explained. But I think those are rather exceptional circumstances and in most cases I think one should adopt a more experimental attitude and try to see what comes out of trusting one's best guess concerning the near future. This needs to be done with the appropriate hedges but without being tied to Professor McCracken's fixed rules. I think that the weaknesses of the fiscal and monetary policies of the postwar period have to do not so much with failure to observe a stable rule than with something Arthur Smithies pointed out, namely, that different groups of experts and of policymakers were hedging in a very one-sided way. In the past few years I think there was a very one-sided hedging against the consequences of unemployment and no hedging against overheating the economy.

In other periods the hedges took different shapes and that, I think, explains the somewhat unstable record which for the postwar period as a whole has not been at all bad.

Rather than to try to cover the waterfront of the discussion, I would like to confine my comments to three or four points. Two are fairly routine, but two are somewhat more important. On the question of the full-employment surplus as an innovation, the innovation is in the factoring of this concept and related estimates into official discussions and official documents. It is not the concept itself. Professor Smithies is absolutely right that this really goes back to Beardsley Ruml.

Secondly, it is perfectly true that an estimate of something like the full-employment budget carries with it a certain amount of vagueness. I don't, however, consider this to be really a fundamental issue. We have a lot of statistics that have a certain underpinning of vagueness that we nonetheless use, and use effectively. I suspect that we can do a better job using the data than ignoring them—even with their infirmities.

Now, to the two major points. I see no conflict between the concept that there ought to be a more clearcut flight plan to guide the basic course of economic policy. and the concept that there will have to be for a great many reasons continuing policy actions and adjustments. A wide array of things will come into the picture from time to time. The general policy strategy that I was pursuing here does not in the slightest extent suggest that somehow or other you set the dials and then you just leave and you don't change anything.

I don't see any conflict here whatsoever. Indeed, with a more clearcut and explicit flight plan we can have a more sophisticated operation than if we just try to *ad hoc* our way along with a very blurred concept as to what ought to constitute par for the course. I think that is absolutely fundamental in this discussion.

Now, to a somewhat more positive note. I think one of the most important critical comments that has been made here this morning, and it is one to which I would subscribe thoroughly, was made by Professor Smithies. At times the government may have to pursue quite consciously "destabilizing" actions in a certain sense because of certain other problems that may arise. For example, it may have to pursue restrictive measures for a time that in the short run may have the effect of increasing unemployment because of developments on the external scene or wage-price problems. We have a multiplicity of objectives. Sometimes one is more important than the other. Sometimes, therefore, we have to move a little one way or the other to take cognizance of this and I think that point is very well taken.

Just one comment to Henry Wallich. I would have called Charlie Schultze before the President did. And also I would have let Charlie publish his estimate, at least implicitly in the budget; I wouldn't have put one in the Economic Report.

Second, to Arthur Smithies. The National Bureau has always been interested in econometric models, and may do more with them in the future. But it isn't going to abandon its other work—not yet anyway. Indeed, I would go on to say that the kind of business-cycle research the Bureau has been doing and is doing is essential for improvement in econometric models. The one won't displace the other.

Questions from the Floor

Comment by Professor David McCord Wright, Department of Economics, University of Georgia: I am worried that, in this excellent presentation, there does not seem to me to have been sufficient mention of international problems. In this connection, I would question whether stable prices for the United States were necessarily a sign of successful policy. For example, it seems to me a very good case could be made out that the failure to let prices rise in the United States in the 1920s was a major precipitant to the international monetary collapse that followed, and it is just possible that a failure to let prices go down now in the United States may have a lot to do with further unstabilizing international developments. I don't think we here in this country even realize the extent to which our policies affect, and are affected by, the economic stability of the world and our need to think out our economic policy not just nationally but internationally.

Professor Meltzer: I have one very brief comment. As I listened to Bob Stone, I thought he described extremely well the reasons why monetary rules, however imperfect they may be, are almost certain to do better than discretion. The policy you describe as a policy of accommodating demand is the one Karl Brunner and I have accused the Federal Reserve of following. It is a restatement of the "real bills" doctrine and it explains why the Federal Reserve reinforces the cycle, encouraging recession when unemployment is rising or expected to rise. You have described, adequately, what the Federal Reserve did in 1966 and in almost every other critical period in monetary history. It supplied more money when prices were expected to rise and less money when prices were expected to fall. The reason it behaves in this way is, I think, precisely the reason you gave. It supplies reserves and base money when the market demands them at the prevailing interest rate and withdraws them when the market rates fall. To avoid these errors Paul McCracken suggests that there be guidelines and Milton Friedman suggests that there be rules for monetary policy. Either of these suggestions would serve us better than the policy that you and your colleagues or former colleagues serve up to us.

PART III

OBJECTIVES OF FISCAL AND BUDGET POLICIES

C. LOWELL HARRISS*

A SUBJECT AS broad as this defies adequate treatment by a long book, let alone a brief paper. Mine will range broadly but leave much untouched and nothing completed.

Introduction: Government Spending

The objective of budget policy is to do what people want. Governments exist to serve people—the federal government to serve everyone in the country.[1] Such observations may seem trite and obvious, but they often share the not uncommon fate of the obvious, being overlooked. Among those who are sometimes guilty of ignoring the "basic"—that the job of government is to do what people want—are professors speaking from a rostrum. How tempting to focus on what the people "ought"

---

*Views are my own and not necessarily those of any organization with which I am associated.

[1] Each state budget, of course, serves fewer. But states as a group, and local governments in combination, serve virtually the same total public as the federal government. Expenditures abroad, and taxes on foreign activities, differentiate slightly the geographical coverage of our national government from that of the totality of states and localities. The whole and the sum of the parts, however, are not the same as regards the practical capacity to tax and spend.

to want, or what the speaker would like to see! The public may have values different from those which we high-minded academicians would like to assume. If this realization is not a little sobering as one contemplates goals, another thought may be: The means available to achieve objectives must affect the attainable and thus the objectives which can wisely be selected—a subject referred to later.

Two other points deserve explicit note because, though almost obvious, they get too little attention: (1) Whatever is done by government is done by people, by human beings with all their strengths and limitations. (2) Most efforts of Americans devoted to achieving objectives are not directed through government as an agency, institution, or means for accomplishing individual or group desires. Production, for the most part, results from what we do privately—in the market. Most consumption is even more private. Collective desires exist, of course, and they are not always distinguishable from the purely personal, a fact of rather distressing complexity in defining the objectives we seek through government.

A symposium on taxation cannot really deal with the growth of expenditures. Yet tax problems as such would be of rather less concern if federal spending had grown less rapidly. The President's budget for the coming fiscal year, 1968, proposes for *non*-defense purposes *per capita* spending (in dollars of 1966 consumer purchasing power) $208 *greater* than that 10 years ago.[2] The *tax rise* to pay for a decade's *growth* of non-defense spending will be over $1,000 for a family of five.

The Making of Choices—What objectives, then, do we seek through the use of national government? Good and not-so-good reasons, often in a mixture which is anything but clear, account for using government instead of other agencies to achieve objectives. At one end of a spectrum are things we *cannot* do privately through business organizations, philanthropy and nonprofit-oriented agencies, and households. National defense, the conduct of foreign affairs, the operation of the monetary mechanism, and the regulation of interstate commerce are examples. Other things we are *not willing* to do pri-

---

[2] The calculations are for the cash budget. The *per capita* rise in defense outlays appears as $75 (in 1966 dollars) over the decade. C. Lowell Harriss. *The Budget of 1968*, Manufacturers Hanover Trust Co., February, 1967.

vately, at least not to the extent that many of us wish, include welfare assistance to the needy, while quite a different case appears in the provision of transportation facilities. The analysis and the argumentation generally involve specific matters with little attention for the total effect of many programs, each having many ramifications. One current tendency, not least among academicians, is to conclude that if something seems worth doing it must be worth doing through the federal government.

As one objective—one element of "budget policy"—I suggest the improvement of procedures *for finding what people want*. With limited resources for satisfying wants, Americans must choose among alternatives. Which services and transfer payments do we value most highly? And in what relative amounts? In buying and selling in the marketplace we "vote" many times a day. These votes indicate preferences; they rank priorities. The alternatives are repriced as the combinations of conditions of supply and demand change. The market process not only permits, but compels the evaluation of alternatives by the persons directly involved.[3] The market process permits more or less continuous adaptation of the myriads of shifting elements so that much adjustment takes place in small amounts. Decisions on federal spending are made rather differently. The people to be served, or not served, have little *direct* participation. Those who will bear the taxes have even less opportunity to guide the decisions on spending. Perhaps the system is as good as is reasonably possible. I suggest, however, that the search for ways to improve expenditure decisions deserves a place on the agenda of a broadly oriented study of federal policy.

New Federal Programs—An unpublished tabulation by the Tax Foundation identifies some 40 new nondefense federal programs in 1966 and 1967 and nearly 100 since early 1961; moreover, many of those functioning in 1960 have been enlarged in ways other than the mere expansion of spending on

---

[3] Private actions affect "third parties" who have no voice in the decisions. One reason given to support government (rather than market) performance of a function is that the interests of third parties can—and presumably will—be taken into account more adequately by the political, than by the market, process. Needless to say, realizing the potentiality requires rather more effort than can be counted upon to be forthcoming.

what was then being done. Almost 20 new nondefense programs are proposed in the budget for 1968. One feels old-fashioned, out-of-step in today's parade, in asserting that each element of federal spending should serve the interests of *everyone* in the country.[4] Extreme—even as an objective? Perhaps. But if one rejects it, why? The cost is borne by a federal tax system which burdens everyone. This latter fact makes for much difficulty in justifying programs of less than national benefit.

The concept of "national interest" presents not a few difficulties. Identification of what really benefits the whole society is not always evident. Measurement of magnitudes will always be highly perplexing. A program which clearly benefits some people does not necessarily serve the public welfare even abstracting from the sacrifices resulting from the necessary taxes. Scores of the programs instituted in recent years seem to me to have rather parochial and limited benefits. In a world of interdependence, of course, one can always envision connections between the small group and the collectivity. Yet as particular federal programs get more detailed, the interests of 200 million Americans in this, that, and the other one become tenuous and remote. These relations are not unlike those third-party elements for which the market (and taxation) fails to take adequate account. To say the least, any justification for federal undertaking of an activity gets weaker as the program gets more specific.

Does anyone now argue seriously that federal spending must really serve everyone? He would be hard to find. Not even the present concern for reducing poverty has shocked us into cessation of federal spending to raise the price of food. Nevertheless, I submit, budgetary policy should seek more earnestly than is currently the fashion to spend where the benefits are spread as broadly as the tax system. As spending becomes more specific, as it deals with more types of activities, the problem of serving the entire public becomes increasingly complex. Tax rate reduction seems to me to offer relatively greater attractions as a means of achieving the myriad of objectives of tens of millions of Americans. Of course, no one can "know";

---

[4] One clear exception exists when service charges or fees paid by the beneficiaries defray the cost.

and the appeal of visible government action seems to have more attraction than reliance upon people acting privately.

The question of the kind of society being built needs to be faced. The cumulative effect of more programs, and even larger total amounts, will have implications for the future which do not enter decision making for the separate units. Perhaps the objective most deserving of current attention is the advance, as contrasted with the narrowing of personal freedom. Taxes limit us in many ways, of course. Yet so do federal outlays—obviously in some cases, but often more subtly. How many Americans have been "kicked around" by highway and urban renewal programs? How are businesses and state-local governments affected by the proliferation of federal spending? When actions of Uncle Sam, that is the men acting in his name with dollars more or less at their discretionary disposal, touch us at so many different points, how does the quality of life become altered? Such questions seem to me to warrant lots more sober thought than they generally receive. The fundamental issue has not been settled when a large group decides that some expenditure would be a "good thing." The real question is whether it is the best alternative possible. The federal tax system is pervasive. One way to help everyone is to reduce tax rates.[5]

To repeat, how can we build an apparatus for dealing well with federal expenditure decisions, for determining what people want most? Not the least of our needs today is clearer indication of the alternatives. How can we choose most effectively?

Objectives and Instruments: Ends and Means

Objectives—of individuals and of groups—are of many types. Some are life's ultimate goals as nearly as a mortal can express them. Affection, health, beauty, security, excitement, peace, hope, humor, graciousness, companionship, honor, and so on. Other things which we sometimes call ends or objectives are in a more accurate sense means. One thinks of them properly as intermediate, to be judged on the basis of their effectiveness

---

[5] The personal income tax falls on almost every family. And does not everyone as a consumer bear some of the employer's payroll tax for social security and some corporation income tax?

in serving more basic goals. To simplify life, we may so elevate some means as to give them the status of ends. Yet doing so can misguide policy. Low interest rates, budget balance, and retaining gold are examples of objectives which have no inherent importance. If they are desirable, the reasons must be found in whatever they help achieve.[6] Much the same applies to reducing cyclical instability. World peace and personal health, though of course means to many ends, come close to what I have in mind as final goals. Neither this country nor any other, except to some extent in time of war, will have an explicit, clearly articulated, formulation of collective objectives. For all its merits, the Employment Act of 1946 does not formulate a *set* of goals. No consensus emerges, nothing clear enough to indicate how to resolve hard questions.

Budget decisions now involve *totals* whose magnitudes few of us can cope with as realities. *Changes* from year to year are large enough in relation to changes in other magnitudes of the economy to exert considerable influence. Yet neither the huge totals nor the changes which are feasible can do everything one might like. Society has no instrument for working miracles.

The real resources needed for accomplishment do not necessarily exist. Spending more dollars on a program or project may be essential to get bigger and better results. Yet as a rule dollars are not the only limiting factor. The skilled labor and other real elements will not always be available in quantity to permit large expansion. Such bottlenecks appear, not only in time of rapid expansion during war, but also in recent years, even before Vietnam activities reached their present scale. Antipoverty and urban renewal programs, among others, have encountered limiting factors which dollars alone could not overcome. Our knowledge of how the economy operates has many gaps. Predictions cannot be counted upon. And so on. The realm of "possible" in "managing" the economy through fiscal (and monetary) policy has many limits—and we are not sure just what they are.

---

[6] A "low" interest rate in itself may seem desirable to the borrower if he can get loans at such a rate, but it will serve him poorly if it reduces supply and thus deprives him of what he wants. In either case, however, the owner of a savings account will be less impressed by the glories of low interest rates.

Full Employment

"Full," "maximum" or "high" employment—"low" or "minimum" unemployment—will appear generally, as to me, to be of prime importance as an objective of federal government policy. To some extent this objective is almost a final end. But more, it is so powerful as a *means* as to command high priority in any ranking of goals of federal policy.[7]

Undesired idleness of men and women, and of their non-human possessions, means loss of attainable income. Any avoidable deprivation of material well-being is bad in itself. In a poor world or country— and ours will not soon be one of plenty—such losses are so obviously evil that further condemnation should need no underlining. More, however, remains to be said. For many people, certainly, idleness brings loss of human dignity and of personal satisfaction. These qualities, though falling in a different scale from money equivalent, are very much part of the whole which should command attention. The value of meaningful activity must rank high for many of us.

Nevertheless, despite the obvious desirability of full employment as a goal, some commentary is in order.

1. Does the public *really* endorse what is *really* at issue? The answer has troublesome implications. Governmental policies depend to some extent upon popular support. And experience of the last dozen years suggests a distressing thought: A public almost "fully" employed—95 percent or so—may have little enthusiasm for acting to do better on this score, to raise employment (or reduce unemployment) by one percentage point. That single point and the billions of national product it represents may seem rather important to an economist, and highly so to the million or more workers and family members directly affected. The vast majority of the public, however, will probably not be much concerned. The problem will appear remote and of rather low order of urgency. Far more people would be hurt by inflation than could themselves benefit from job expansion.

2. Both the *definition* and *measurement* of "unemployment" and of such concepts as "plant capacity" and "labor force" need

---

[7] State-local governments have quite different powers and responsibilities as regards employment.

further improvement. This point has been made often. "Hidden" unemployment can be very real but very elusive to measure and deal with. Less widely recognized, and far from any prospect of being met, is the need for data on *unfilled jobs*. The closer the economy comes to full utilization of resources, the greater the difficulties of measuring what we *then* need to know. What is then at issue are small differences, requiring precision of measurement.

3. Causes of unemployment sometimes seem clear and obvious. When unemployment reaches low levels, however, when job vacancies become relatively numerous, the reasons for the unemployment which remains are probably complex. At least, the causes become more difficult to deal with satisfactorily. Debates over the last few years have helped to clarify the nature and the relative importance of "aggregate demand" and "structural" forces. I add only one comment: Discussions of causes of unemployment often omit an element of no small significance—the wage rate. Sometimes today one feels hopelessly out of the swim by insisting that "labor"—in the aggregate and in particular industries and companies—can price itself out of work. Yet is it not obvious that $750 billion of final demand (for the constituents of GNP) will buy fewer manhours at an average wage rate of $3.20 than at one of $3? The relation of wage rates to cost-push inflation, to general and specific unemployment, to creeping inflation—and to public policy generally—must warrant concern. At issue may be the key to one of the most difficult problems of aggregate economic policy. Here, certainly, we encounter one reason why policies to achieve major objectives raise conflicts.

4. Full employment in itself has costs. Labor shortages create difficulties for those who cannot readily, by paying more, get what they want as promptly as otherwise—whether a taxi, nursing service, repairs, or manufactured products. Although total output and income exceed what would otherwise be, some disadvantages result, some costs which escape measurement.[8] Time taken to fill jobs goes up.

5. Near-term and somewhat longer-run considerations do

---

[8] The costs which are reflected in measures of the price level will be taken into account in deflating GNP and other money measures of aggregate performance.

not necessarily harmonize. One hesitates to suggest that business recession is anything but evil. Perhaps, however, periods of economic slack—of unemployment which monetary and fiscal policy could eliminate—help prepare conditions for higher employment (at any given level of prices) later.

Avoidance of Inflation

Employment, useful activity, has human value. Price-level stability in and of itself cannot claim comparable merit. Yet both price-level stability and employment are means to ends beyond themselves. Price-level changes, the contrast to stability, affect (a) the total of real output and (b) the way it is shared—both matters of true significance. To me it seems that the objective of price stability deserves more respect than economists generally accord it. Time does not permit even a brief discussion of those complex and imperfectly understood processes—the *causes* and the *effects* of changes in price levels. Budget policy, if I may be assertive, has less independent significance for price-level change than is frequently implied; the results depend heavily upon monetary developments which are subject to separate controls. Nevertheless, decisions about the federal budget properly attach weight to price-level stability if only because federal deficits and surpluses have monetary significance.

Perhaps governmental policy pays too much, or too little, attention to "the" price level. In either case, unfortunately, we do not know what "the" price level has been or is. It is worse than a pity that this country has not done more of what is possible to improve price indices. Experts in and outside of government would doubtless agree that some changes which are within our capabilities would be improvements. The merits of other possibilities arouse debate, and some problems defy solution. President Johnson two years ago seemed officially to endorse the widely accepted view that the Consumer Price Index has defects which on balance bias it by around 1.5 percent a year, i.e., if the index number rises 1.5 percent a year the true price level has in fact been unchanged. Perhaps the CPI does have a bias. If so, in what direction and in what probable amount? And if the White House or the BLS knows of the existence of error and has some judgment of the size, why not make corrections? If there is doubt, should not more be done to remove it? This country is rich enough to afford better data on price levels as well as on employment!

In an economy with rigidities and inflexibilities, the forces which lead to a general decline in the price level can also be counted upon to lead to decline in the utilization of labor and other productive capacity.[9] Many wage rates and other prices are inflexible downward, at least for many months and even years. If money demand declines, the quantity of man hours purchased will drop unless wage rates per hour go down. A decline in prices may create expectations of further declines. As a result, some purchases will be postponed, temporarily reducing total demand, perhaps for inventory for the next few weeks, perhaps for new construction over a much longer period. The avoidance of price-level declines seems to me desirable as an objective even though, in principle, some benefits of rising productivity might well be taken in lower prices.

A rise in the general level of prices will hurt some people, benefit others. We have often heard about the effects of inflation on the distribution of income and wealth—especially the loss of purchasing power for persons on fixed incomes. These effects may not be as unqualifiedly bad, or as innocuous, as is sometimes implied. If the choice lies between distributional change brought by price-level increase of, say 2 percent, and a difference in total production equal to that of 1 percent of employment for a year, the latter, the larger output, seems to win. Yet I doubt that in fact such is the real choice. Here, however, my time will be given to results other than those of income and wealth distribution, if only because the latter have been discussed more often.

Other effects of price-level change are less familiar and perhaps less certain. Yet their combined influence can be substantial. Over the long run the accumulated results of inflation on growth, efficiency, and general well-being will be more adverse, and in more ways, than is generally recognized. Let me assert, briefly, dogmatically, and subject to correction:

---

[9] Clearly, my comments here do little more than alert us to the fact that inflation is not the only type of price-level change. The world has seen more than one deflation, and they have had adverse effects.

1. Changes in the general *level* of prices do not work on all prices with the same force and timing. Price *relations* change for reasons other than the working of the forces of real demand and supply in their long-run context. As a result, the efficient conduct of business, and of all economic affairs, becomes more difficult. Rational calculation in the comparison of alternatives becomes harder. Errors otherwise avoidable result.[10] Resource allocation will suffer.

2. The longer-lived an investment or a commitment, the greater will be the danger of error which arises out of changes in either relative prices or the general price level. Calculations can go farther awry if the gap between decision and end-result is 20 years than if it is five and if the price level is changing rather than stable. When the value of the monetary unit is felt to be uncertain not merely when changes actually do occur, some undertakings which would benefit the community will be foregone or curtailed; but there will be others which are made to seem wise in dollar terms because of expected price-level changes, and these undertakings will get relatively more resources than is inherently desirable. Today's best judgments, in other words, will be made wrong by price-level changes which have no basis in underlying, real change in resource availability, technological reality, and consumer tastes.[11]

3. The fact of price-level change, given our tax laws and accounting practices, and uncertainty about the purchasing power of money will, I think, reduce capital accumulation over the long run. Admittedly, the factors relevant to this subject are complex. Not all point unequivocally in the one direction. The saving which is essential for capital growth results from

---

[10] Not all results will be "errors"; some by the laws of chance will be fortunate. But for reasons which space restrictions preclude my developing here, benefits from the disruption of relative prices will not, I believe, approximate the total harm. Certainly, policy cannot wisely be grounded on convictions that advantages will predominate.

[11] For example, if construction and other costs are expected to rise, may it not seem wise to build productive capacity somewhat before the actual need? Some new capacity will then be idle for a few weeks or months or even longer, representing a little waste in the form of unemployment of plant idleness before full utilization. Moreover, building prematurely, by perhaps only a few months will commit the future to reliance upon techniques which are slightly less than the best available when the decision would have been made if business had felt no reason to try to anticipate a price level increase.

many causes and sources whose relations to inflation are obscure and uncertain. The expectation of inflation might conceivably add enough to the attraction of owning equities to stimulate net savings, etc., enough to offset unintended capital consumption (inadequate depreciation) and the effects from discouragement of holding debt. Tax laws and administration might be devised to allow enough deduction for depreciation to keep capital consumption allowances from being labeled "income" for purposes of taxation at high rates. The prospects of such prevention are not promising. Certainly, we are not safe in assuming their existence when it is not a fact.

4. Uncertainty about price-level change will discourage the use of debt contracts. The greater the uncertainty, the greater will be the discouragement of long-term debts for borrowers or lenders or both. Uncertainty is a cost. No one will assume it willingly except for compensation. In debts, the characteristic device for reflecting cost is in the interest charge—a "premium" above some riskless rate.[12] When the time period of a debt is a few months, the effect on interest rates of uncertainty about the price level will be of no great consequence. For as little as five years, however, the magnitude attributable to uncertainty can be significant; for 20 or 40 years the amounts can be of very great moment indeed. Would not interest rates as quoted go up, perhaps by amounts which would seem shockingly large?

What interest-rate *level* is consistent with degrees of uncertainty which lie within the range of probability? Let us try to imagine, for example, an expectation that the price level will probably rise by, say, 1 percent a year but with a considerable possibility that in some years the rise will be 2 percent or more and with only a very slight probability that prices will decline. What terms would you as borrower or lender (a) insist upon and (b) be willing to accept for a 20-year loan or one equal to the life of a new house? The structure of rates would also present problems. What would be the relation of rates for long-run debts to the rate for short-term debt, if people felt that over 20 years the price level might rise as little as 5 percent but might be 15 percent and even 30 percent (1.5 percent a year, not compounded) higher at the end?

---

[12] Any distinction between risk and uncertainty is ignored here.

The use of long-term debt instruments, including leases and other long-term contracts in money terms, would be impaired. Our economy has benefited from the financing of housing and other capital facilities by mortgages and other forms of long-term debt. Expectation of price-level uncertainty would impede rather than help the use of debt with duration more or less in line with the life of productive capacity, including housing, which has great significance.

5. The record of inflation in the past, its presence currently, and any serious expectation that the price level is going to rise in the future, will be likely to encourage or cause unemployment. The belief that a little inflation is a low price to pay for fuller employment has wide acceptance. But it does not reflect the realistic choice before this country. Both price-level increases and the expectation of more, I fear, are likely to lead to some wage-rate rises which are greater than would otherwise occur. If so—and one cannot predict with confidence —such action will price some man-hours into idleness. The process can be gradual, indirect, and utterly impossible to isolate. Much will depend upon the visibility of prices and other factors, bargaining power, governmental policy (e.g., boosting minimum wage rates), etc. The "remedy" will be money creation to "validate" the higher wage rate.[13]

6. Another reason for setting price-level stability as an objective overlaps much of what has been said so far. It is not easily expressed in terms concrete, realistic, and responsible. Economic life becomes more difficult at many points when price levels change. Two illustrations can be drawn from my own experience: Financing college operations, especially salaries, seems inherently difficult. Much hard effort has accomplished much over several years—at great cost to students and their parents, alumni and other donors, and taxpayers. Yet at this moment, I am sure, problems seem still huge because, in part, faculty members expect an uncertain amount of future infla-

---

[13] This all-too-brief treatment of a somewhat familiar point, but one too rarely spelled out, does not do it justice. Lags complicate the casual interpretation of experience. The monetary and fiscal restraint of the late 1950s and of 1960 may have been costly in terms of unemployment then. But did it not thereby reduce the upward pressure of wage rates during the early 1960s and thus help make possible several years of general expansion without much price-level increase?

tion and seek protection. Treadmills get tiring and thereby make more difficult the rational, sympathetic, efficient solution of human problems of compensation, career commitment, and governmental-private balance in higher education. Wages and salaries loom large in the costs of government. Rarely are there objective criteria for determining "proper" wage rates for even large groups of jobs (police with 10 years of service, elementary school teachers, mail carriers, etc.), to say nothing of particular individuals. Job security and pension systems can lead to long lags in quantity adjustment. The employer's earning record does not help indicate productivity. Quality differences are often obscure. And so on. When the price level has changed and stability appears uncertain, negotiation of new wage rates becomes more than normally difficult. Problems of running the public business get harder as a result of doubts about the future purchasing power of the dollar.

7. The pressures of inflation are likely to invite *direct controls*—the guideline approach converted into something more than "voluntary." Innocuous as some such restraints may seem (at first), narrowly restricted as their original scope, direct controls will not do the job intended unless they do *force* people to act against what they believe to be their advantage. No reasonably foreseeable controls are likely to affect the whole economy very much in the short run, for good or harm. Nevertheless, over any substantial period direct controls can work much damage on the productive system and the social fabric. Yet unless the underlying forces making for inflation are themselves moderated, the realities of inflation will appear at different places and in different forms.[14] Many effects will be concealed and utterly beyond measurement. How can the public possibly learn what would have developed under freer conditions? The differences in production and consumption will be changes for the worse.

8. Balance-of-payments difficulties are aggravated by price-level increases. Ending an upward trend in prices will in itself involve strains and losses. One need not look to the extremes of Brazil or Chile for examples. Our own experience of the

---

[14] At the risk of excessive oversimplification, I suggest that for the long run any anti-inflationary successes will result from those direct controls which keep (a) growth of the quantity of money and (b) velocity of circulation below what would otherwise be the case.

late 1950s shows how efforts to exercise the devil of inflation can prove costly.

Distribution of Burdens and Benefits

When economists write about fiscal objectives, they sometimes try to deal systematically with how the costs of government "ought" to be shared. The results of such theorizing or moralizing may strike men of affairs as a bit naive and lacking in sympathy for the requirements of success. What sense, or nonsense, underlies the conclusion that of two men in as nearly similar positions as definable and receiving the same government services, the one who produces more by working more hours a year must also bear more of the cost of government? The attempts of theorists, however, do often have one characteristic which must command respect: an effort to see things whole. In contrast, much of what most of us say about this feature of the fiscal system and that—the investment credit, depreciation, the foreign tax credit—gives little attention to the significance for the overall distribution of cost of government.

Federal taxes and expenditures will inevitably alter the distribution of "income" and "wealth," both conceived in the very broadest sense as, roughly, "what people want badly enough to make sacrifices to get." "Alter" as used here means changes as compared with what would otherwise result. What would now exist if either the levels or the patterns of federal financing had been greatly different for a decade or so? Speculation to answer such a question offers little promise of satisfying rewards. Starting with the here and now, however, we do have open alternatives involving significant differences about the effects of the fiscal system on the distribution of income and wealth. My own thoughts and feelings would require an extensive paper on what the objectives "ought" to be—in the dream-world sense or in the world of practical reality.[15] And

---

[15] Two examples will illustrate what I have in mind. The real world as I see it includes governors, mayors, and school officials whose combined power will be effective in continuing the exemption of municipal bond interest from federal income tax. The world of reality also leads me to put little hope (or fear) in the prospect of altering the taxation of natural resources to the distress of Texans who have been successful in oil and gas exploration.

the paper I would write today would in some respects differ more than a little from that of a decade ago—and not at all in others. Here I propose a variety of points as bases for possible discussion.

Extremes offer worse than poor bases for determining policy for the general public. Exceptions—of wealth and poverty, of gains ill-gotten and riches used with brilliant creativity, of ingenious ways to use the law while violating the intent—properly deserve consideration. Nevertheless, more often than will be foreseen by the person who focuses on it, the exception when generalized will provide a poor basis for policy affecting the broad public. No easy problem exists here, as the growing complexity of tax law indicates, to say nothing of the startling increase in the number of different spending programs.

Academic writing tends to give much prominence to reducing inequality, *redistribution*, as a goal and identifies it with *vertical equity*. Yet as one poses the standard queries—why, how, what, when, who—in seeking guides to implementation, matters get "sticky." As an objective of policy, what guidance can we find? My own feeling is that a more humane, constructive, and potentially fruitful starting point lies in the goal of *reducing tax burdens on the poor* and near poor. Admittedly, compassion and sympathy for the poor can lead to softness and muddle-headed politics. "Soaking the rich" may have appeal, but not to the best of human values. Somehow, neither it nor less demagogic versions deserve admiration. Yet the qualities found in some discussions of tax burden distribution still embody more of the "anti" spirit than seems to me likely to advance civilization.

The aspect of redistribution as an objective which appeals to me on subjective, emotional, visceral grounds is the "uplift," not the "pull down," emphasis. And is there not also rational and objective basis for preferring this emphasis in public policy? A warning, however: if federal spending is to be as high as is widely advocated, tax burdens on low-income groups will deprive them of funds they can ill-afford to sacrifice. This reality may be ignored, but it cannot be escaped by taxing "business" or imposing high rates where the tax base is narrow. One way to help the family with low income—all such families—is to cut federal tax rates.

An unsophisticated, non-expert observer of federal tax rates would expect a great deal of vertical inequality in actual tax bills. In fact as well as "on the books," much inequality does exist. It may, or may not, be adequate to satisfy our standards of vertical equity; it may be excessive. How can one truly judge even for oneself? Some existing inequality, however, must strike almost anyone as deplorable and some as at least of questionable merit. There are individuals and families with "low" incomes who pay more than do others with significantly larger amounts of what I would call income. Briefly, there remains "unfinished business" in devising a system to achieve any rationally defensible objective of redistribution, reduction of economic inequality.

Justice in the Distribution of Tax Burdens—Modern taxes are not only heavy but must also be unequal in the sense that some people must pay more than will others. When taxes in a democratic society are heavy, unequal, and entail the use of government's power of coercion, one result must be expected: If voters do not feel that the results are at least moderately fair, just, and equitable, social tension and pressure for change will result. The tax system will eventually be modified.

Perhaps that last statement appears somewhat naive.[16] If so, perhaps another will seem more realistic: Tax proposals which do not seem to be fair will have decidedly less possibility of adoption than will those which appear as being equitable. In popular discussions of taxation, do any considerations have greater emotional impact than "fairness" and "unfairness"?[17] Feelings, however, do not always correspond to well formulated bases in logic and ethics. Although tax change may not require an extensive foundation of popular support, even a strong leader will have difficulty if his tax proposals violate

---

[16] Judging the quality and depth of public feelings about taxes must be hazardous. One can easily get disturbed by the apparent indifference of the voter to oft-mentioned crudities and inequalities. Dealing with them is compounded by frustration at the complexities which must be faced in dealing with them.

[17] The "unfairness" which gets into law and administration often results because someone wants the particular results. Not surprisingly, one finds private endorsement of special features which favor some taxpayers but which others can find little reason to support on grounds of fairness for the general public.

142

the popular sense of justice. Unquestionably, fairness must be an objective of federal tax policy. To achieve it, we must continue efforts to clarify the concept, to build a broader consensus on both the meaning of what we seek and then how it can be achieved. Neither is easy, neither insuperable. One obvious difficulty is that other considerations do not always lend themselves to what seems called for in meeting goals of justice.[18]

Concern over horizontal equity, over the equality and inequality in burden distribution among families in about the same income (and wealth) class, calls for unending attention. For one reason or another, tax bills on individuals and families can be made to differ according to circumstances which have much, or little, relevance to support costs of government. Reasonable men can clarify the issues and in trying to do so will provide the makings of progress. The same applies to the search for vertical equity as distinguished from attempts at redistribution as such. How much of what will bring how much difference in sharing the cost of government? Good question. But who today will be willing to devote the time needed for the analysis which high tax rates warrant? Some academicians. Some researchers, in and out of government. Given the importance of what is at stake, however, the current concern seems deplorably small.

Should visibility be an explicit objective of fiscal policy? Government, the "peoples' business," is big by any measure, e.g., per capita federal taxes or spending. Much goes along largely unseen, unnoticed, merely taken for granted. We find it far easier in some cases than in others to judge which individuals are affected by a form of spending or by a tax—and by how much.[19] Presumably, awareness will be conducive to better choices than will ignorance. The vast public "business"

---

[18] Per dollar of revenue, "business" taxes can be relatively inexpensive to administer or appear as hidden. By reasonable standards, however, they can be distinctly inequitable.

[19] For a recent study of evidence, see *Tax Burdens and Benefits of Government Expenditures by Income Class, 1961 and 1965*, (New York: Tax Foundation, 1967). Debates over tax shifting continue. Doubt about the eventual resting place of some taxes remains among those who study the theory and the evidence. Taxes on corporation income and business payrolls (for social security) present some of the chief difficulties.

which so affects each person's life does not get directed or executed by God. Human beings decide on the policies and then do what is done—for the whole society. Ours, of course, is a representative government. We choose people to act for us in setting policy. There is no expectation that each person will participate even indirectly in decision making which affects him. Yet how much insulation is desirable?

Hidden taxes conceal the costs of government from the persons who pay. In using such revenue sources, society sacrifices one instrument which can help, at least marginally, in making better, rather than poorer, decisions. So it seems to me, at least. One must be more cautious, however, in generalizing about federal finances than about those near home. The influences determining federal expenditures are complex. And is there not merit in arrangements which free us from worry about taxes? Specialization, the division of labor, peace of mind are all served by delegation of responsibility for deciding problems of federal finances.

No extensive popular participation information of tax laws and in the decisions on spending is possible, and I cannot conceive of the results of any such attempt. What are the alternatives, however? At a minimum, I suggest, we do well to support the principle of selecting taxes which are sufficiently evident to enable, or force, the taxpayer to relate costs to expenditures.

Economic Growth

Alexander Hamilton and Albert Gallatin, to go back a bit in history, made economic growth explicit goals of federal fiscal policy. The nineteenth century tariff debates reflected differences in views about how taxing power could be used to encourage growth. Andrew Mellon's years of work to reduce the first World War tax rates rested on his belief that doing so would facilitate economic progress. In short, as we assign economic growth a place among fiscal policy goals, we are not innovating but continuing a practice as old as the republic. Our world, of course, is different and neither old reasons nor old methods are necessarily best for today. Why, however, use coercion as expressed through government action to try to achieve economic growth?

144

One matter involves definition. As with the terms applying to other objectives of fiscal policy—"full employment," "price level," "tax fairness"—definition of "economic growth" as a guide for public policy presents problems. Perhaps we do not go far wrong in using the familiar GNP and concluding that when it gets bigger the economy has grown in the sense we wish. But who can know? Clearly, allowances must be made for price-level change. And other problems involve more than esoteric debate among specialists. Comparison from one year to the next will deal with matters which are predominantly comparable. Over 10 years or so, however, comparability suffers.[20]

In specifying "growth" as an objective, we, by definition, say that we want something better than would come from achievement of the "full employment" objective alone, the full use of today's productive capacity. The precise content of the "betterness," unfortunately, cannot be entirely clear. Some wants satisfied more adequately will be collective (social), some more clearly private. They may be larger output (including better quality), lower cost per unit of output (more desired leisure then adding to real output), or some combination. Economic growth involves the years, the decades, the generations. In making fiscal decisions for the long run, do the considerations which are properly weighted heavily differ from those which dominate the short run?

One fact can be pointed out at once: The market place cannot reflect today the preferences of future Americans. Consumer and investor sovereignty may not have quite the merit we attribute to them for allocating resources today. Society does have means, notably the family, for recognizing somehow, and somewhat, the interests of those who—being too young or unborn—are now too weak to protect themselves. Another

---

[20] A fundamental deficiency of GNP as a measure of accomplishment is the arbitrary valuation of what government does. The dollar taken by taxation (coercion) is assumed to have the same value as the dollar paid out freely in buying in the market. The spending of the government dollar (except for transfer) is assumed to bring a dollar of benefit for someone, identity not clear. No better accounting treatment may be possible. But this one may seem unsatisfactory for one particular purpose of special concern here—the role of taxation and government spending in economic growth. At the least, caution is in order.

instrument for doing so may be national government. The men
and women voting today may, more or less deliberately, use
federal finances to benefit the future at the sacrifice of the present. I assume that no Santa Claus will provide means of doing
more for the future without need to sacrifice something today.
Note my verb, "may." What does the record indicate? Have
national government decisions involving a long-time horizon
—for example, disposition of the federal public domain in the
nineteenth century—been generally better than those made
privately? How does one weight markedly different kinds of
actions? And looking to the future, are there convincing a
priori reasons to believe that from now on national government actions with a long-time perspective will be better or
poorer than in the past, and as compared with the private sector? Note that someone today will probably be worse off, and
the losses may be worth more than the benefits in the future—
the childless widow with cancer might weight next year more
highly than a more bountiful 1980.

What can federal fiscal policy do to aid or hinder growth?[21]
Means and ends get intertwined, but one can distinguish between policies which affect the quantity of productive capacity
and those which influence the efficiency of allocation and the
effectiveness of resource utilization. The latter will probably
benefit us today as well as our children.

Budget policy can be adapted deliberately in an effort to increase or reduce the rate of capital accumulation — tangible
capital only or tangible plus human. The recipe, however, must
be rather more complex than is sometimes assumed. A dollar
more of federal tax collections does not necessarily lead to more
capital accumulation than otherwise results. And when it does,
the net addition may not be worth a dollar. But space limits
force me to stop at this point.

The subject of resource allocation[22] and economic growth as
policy objectives warrants an entire paper. Budget policy on
the expenditure side deals, and deals explicitly, with not only

---

[21] My own conclusions as of some years ago were summarized in two
articles each almost as long as the space available to me here.

[22] Time has not permitted me to develop the argument as it applies to
special tax impediments, e.g., Interest Equalization Tax.

aggregates—the "macro" aspects of economics, but also with specific and particular "micro" elements some of which are designed to achieve growth. Federal tax policy does the same. Both might attempt more in this direction. Preferable policy, however, would seem to me to make tax laws more general, reducing rather than enlarging differentiation. Here the objective resembles somewhat that of curtailing rather than enlarging the number of spending programs.

The principle of seeking general application of tax laws will be endorsed widely, but action involves "specifics." They attract concentrated attention which far outweighs in practical effect the influence of a principle. High tax rates, in one sense, create an opportunity. A barrier which is high can be lowered for those who do something especially desired. The possibility of utilizing such opportunity will increasingly seem acceptable, or even the right way to run society, as tax laws include more and more differentiation. Provisions which reduce a tax obstacle are sometimes called "tax incentives." The term does not always seem apt. But terminology counts for little compared with fact. What are the facts? The *tax* structure can affect the *economic structure*—especially so if *differences* in taxes are substantial.

During the war and postwar years of very high tax rates more than one country has achieved more than one objective by the offer of opportunities to escape from very high tax burdens. Some of the objectives have unquestionably been worthy. But were they the most worthy? How can anyone judge with confidence? What would have happened otherwise? Perhaps some sectors and activities which received no favoritism would have been more desirable than parts of those which were undertaken. With any given amount of revenue loss possible, general reduction in tax rates on business seems to me better for the long run than more concentrated reductions at a few points. I include even the investment credit in the object of my criticism here. If for revenue or other reasons, higher tax burdens are required, adverse discriminations are subject to criticism as compared with equal application. Why?

In general, special tax provisions are inconsistent with an element required for optimum efficiency, for the best in resource allocation. Such provisions introduce an element of coercion rather than free choice to influence decisions about *what* to produce, *how, where, when,* and *for whom*. The choices thus being made are to some extent influenced by persons not parties to the transactions, and, by lawmakers and administrators. Opportunities are altered for reasons which reflect votes in the ballot box and then, perhaps, only very, very indirectly. The determinants do not follow from economic choices expressed by the means for conveying them, e.g., dollars in the market. Each of us, I expect, could suggest ways in which the allocation of resources would be better. Housing would appeal to A; faster modernization of factories would please B; C's top priority might go to the arts, while D would be unable to decide between reduction of water pollution and better airports. Each means well for the whole society and feels confident that his proposal will serve the general interest.

Good intentions, however, are not enough, not even when supported by the confidence that one has "the answer." In using taxation or government expenditure, the political process must be used in selecting both the ends and the means. This process inevitably brings into the decision making men with no special competence for the specific problem. How many will have an informed judgment about the comparative results of the relevant alternatives? Moreover, men whose interests differ widely are involved; their power also differs widely, as much so as where dollars rule in the marketplace. The compromises which are inevitable can hardly be assumed to be those for dealing with society's problems.[23] A priori, I suggest, special features are more general features of equal revenue (or spending) amount.

Nor should one overlook the practical problems of keeping up to date. The resource allocation which is best for one time or place will become less nearly ideal as conditions change. Obsolescence may come suddenly and strikingly. More often it

---

[23] Obviously, I oversimplify, failing to distinguish broad issues of allocation between the government sector and the private economy, which only the political process can accomplish, from the more specific detailed matters which get into granting tax favors for this, relative penalties for that. The injection of a variety of economic issues into politics complicates the truly important job of solving society's essentially political problems.

creeps up, not appearing with the dramatic force needed to command attention and compel action. Removal, or even adaptation to changing conditions, will almost always be difficult, and perhaps verge on the impossible. The 1933 "special provisions for depreciation," lasted quite a time! Society ought to do better than we can count upon in keeping tax laws up to date. For any given amount of revenue the allocation distortions, I believe, will be fewer when the effective tax rates are the same over all industry than when differentials are appreciable.

Special provisions of an "incentives" type have an often-noted disadvantage. Their "cost" tends to be high.[24] Legislatures as a rule have no way to limit tax concessions to those actions which are truly additional, those which would not be taken except for the special tax provision. For the marginal (incremental) benefit obtained, the public may pay rather dearly when the method used consists of granting tax favors to *all* in the general class even though the group may not be large.[25] Meanwhile, other objectives also desirable at the margin not only get no tax stimulus but go without benefit of lower tax rates which would otherwise be possible. Thus, while some results of special tax incentives may be dramatically impressive, the alternatives sacrificed rarely appear. How, then, can the public judge the true costs? Resource misallocation from special features of federal tax law will probably not, over the long run, impose huge costs on the economy and retard eco-

---

[24] When government buys office supplies or motor fuel, it pays for what it gets and for no more. When it tries to get something by granting a tax concession, however, it may "pay for" more than it gets. Suppose, for example, that lawmakers agree that the public interest will be served by enlarging investment in small businesses. Unquestionably, a tax concession can stimulate such investment. The favor is granted, therefore—but to all such investment. The public accords the favor to every company in the general class, including firms which in any case would have acted just about as they did. For what may be only a modest additional investment of the kind desired, society "pays" as well for those amounts which would have appeared without the tax concession.

[25] The frame of reference should be "per dollar of revenue." The significant magnitudes change as time passes. One need only think, for example, of the relative size of different groups of savings institutions and other financial intermediaries in the 1930s and the same groups in the 1960s.

nomic growth appreciably. But who can say? And why take the chance? [26]

Relations to Other Economies

Tariff debates in the past, and more recently gold flows and the tax treatment of foreign income, have related federal financial policies directly to the ties between our domestic economy and other parts of the world. The connections are more numerous than can be discussed here. Their nature and importance differ vastly.

Most foreign trade and investment is conducted privately. Why is there governmental interest of a sort to involve fiscal policy? A complete answer would take us far afield. At one extreme are matters inherently governmental. Keeping the peace is almost as nearly an end in itself as anything imaginable — but not quite, as our record even today in the Far East demonstrates. Other goals are more nearly means than ends desirable in themselves, e.g., achieving balance in international accounts. There is no inherent reason why government must get involved, and life might be better if there were no such involvement. But government is concerned. No one economy can be master of its own fate—including the conditions under which its subjects deal with foreigners. By playing a part a few governments can force others to act where, if free, they would prefer nonintervention.

The use of federal spending power, other than the rather minor costs of diplomacy, to achieve international objectives is relatively new in our history. Foreign aid comes to mind. The goals are mixed, and their merit disputed; the amount that can be accomplished with dollars and the most effective ways of using them are also debated. In contrast, the use of the *taxing*

---

[26] The use of special provisions will distort the incentive system. If the adoption (or elimination) of such detailed features is the way things are done, then persons potentially affected will act accordingly. A manager trying to serve the owners of a corporation will feel compelled to work industriously for special provisions which would aid his particular company in preference to tax rate reduction (of equal total revenue) to be shared by all corporations. Does he not have a clear bias? The resulting incentive structure tends to favor trying to get tax burdens reduced by adding to the list of elements that involve the proliferation of special features. These pile up their distorting, complicating, and deceiving consequences.

power is as old as tariff history. Nonrevenue objectives over-shadowed revenue considerations in Hamilton's day and do so now in the Geneva negotiations. Regarding taxation, two relatively recent concerns warrant comment.

Congress has considered recently the taxation of foreign business activities and of income from abroad. Why? What problems exist and what objectives are sought? One conflict will illustrate. Other countries have tax systems which differ from ours. Americans operating there may be subject to two sets of taxes involving not only very high burdens if piled on each other but also different sets of rules. Some resolution of conflict, some harmonization, is essential. But more or less than at present? And to what purpose? One plausible objective may be to tax companies operating abroad on the same basis as their foreign competitors, or at least no more heavily. Our government, it may be argued, ought not use its taxing power to impede Americans in taking advantage of opportunities outside our boundaries. In some cases, however, the application of this rule would mean that owners in this country would be treated differently from other U.S. citizens. Many countries tax business (account being taken of their tax treatment of dividends) less heavily than does the United States; in view of this difference, attempts of the United States to grant American companies equality of treatment with their foreign competitors will encourage capital export from the high-tax area, ours. And most of the contribution of the capital to paying for cost of government will remain abroad as our tax credit now operates.

A nagging balance-of-payments problem has persisted for a decade. Can we confidently expect to live well with continued increase in our short-term obligations to foreigners? If not, something needs to be done so that the annual deficit will eventually be eliminated. No one can say for sure just when such a reckoning must be faced. The date can be hastened or postponed by "intangibles," such as confidence (or lack of it) in the purchasing power of the dollar. Or we may end the free sale of gold at $35 per ounce. Amidst many uncertainties, there is one certainty: we cannot count upon existing economic forces to bring a desirable adjustment automatically. The operations of private market forces will not be self-correcting.

Two billion dollars a year seems small in an economy which annually produces more than $750 billion of goods and services. The adjustments needed to deal with a domestic dislocation of this size could be made without obvious strains and difficulties. Small price changes and a little reallocation of resources would do the job. When foreign trade and finance are involved, however, the adjustment is more difficult. Government has a part to play, and fiscal policy inevitably bears on the problem. One reason for difficulties which seem to call for government involvement is that reactions abroad bear upon the result and may work in the wrong way. For another, inflexibilities associated with government retard adjustment.[27] Consequently, the problem we face is relatively greater than its dollar magnitude might indicate. To repeat, the problem is not likely to be solved by free markets. But why seek a solution?

Our basic objective—beyond world peace, the preservation of freedom, and humanitarian concern for the world's poor —is to be able to import. Yet there are additional objectives. One is to maintain broad markets which permit economies of scale and which make for competition over broad areas. Failure to solve the long-standing problem of the deficit could eventually bring a sharp break, some sudden large strain might find Americans unable to meet obligations to foreigners. Our ability to import would then decline. More probable would be the growth of direct controls on trade and investment, with proliferating evils. Our government began several years ago to cut down the dollar drain which results from federal spending itself; most foreign aid spending has been concentrated in this country, and military agencies have been required to do more and more of their buying in this country even though the cost is higher than in foreign lands. To greater extent than we like to admit openly, Uncle Sam in his military buying and foreign aid is trying to achieve the results which would follow from a devaluation of the dollar.

---

[27] Two are especially important. (a) Inflexible exchange rates, between the dollar and the pound, franc, mark, and other currencies, etc., insulate producers and consumers in different countries from forces which would otherwise operate to alter prices, output, and consumption. (b) Central banks no longer permit gold movements to have the internal equilibrating effects which once worked to help restore balance-of-payments equilibrium and thus to end gold flows.

Federal taxation has been called into play. The Interest Equalization Tax acts as a selective devaluation of the dollar. The Revenue Act of 1962 reduced what had been tax disparity favoring investment abroad, especially by leaving business profits in other countries.[28] During the 1963-64 debates on tax reduction, the Kennedy-Johnson Administrations argued that rate reductions would help meet the balance-of-payments problem. There were skeptics then, and some of their doubts have not been dispelled. Expansion of production means rising imports of raw materials. Consumers use part of their higher incomes to buy more imported goods. Rising domestic demand cuts down the availability of items for export and tends to reduce the need and desire to press sales in foreign markets.[29] The tax reduction of 1964 was followed by some price rises (no causal relation being implied here). As U.S. goods and services became a little more expensive, foreigners grew somewhat less willing and able to buy our products. The same change made the problem of foreign suppliers selling here easier.[30]

Taxes affect the international competitive position by influencing production costs, directly and indirectly. In this connection, a good deal depends upon the relative size of taxes on businesses as such. A government has some leeway to alter prices by the structure of taxes it imposes as well as by their level. Moreover, the tax obstacles or incentives to introduce cost-cutting, modern machinery can make some differences in prices. But I now get rather too far from objectives into means. Capital is a highly important means of course. We want it

---

[28] Balance-of-payments considerations were not the only, and not necessarily the chief, considerations back of the foreign tax provision of the 1962 law.

[29] Will not foreigners with more dollars step up purchases here? Some other economies may have "ample" gold and dollar reserves so that if we buy more from them their residents do not buy correspondingly more from us, at least in the short run. In other cases, however, all the dollars that become available from our buying abroad will be used to buy here. If so, a rise in our imports will be matched roughly, by an increase in exports which would not otherwise take place.

[30] Price-level changes in other countries, of course, affect our relative position. In the last two or three years most other major economies have experienced greater rises in their price levels than has the U.S.

where it will serve us best, whether here or abroad.[31] But when it leaves, the record shows up on the "wrong" side of the accounts of an economy with a balance-of-payments deficit. How much can taxes affect capital flows? In what ways? Once again, forces operate in ways too complex and obscure to be dealt with adequately here. A tax cut, however, will improve business profits and tend to make the economy more attractive for capital, especially if rates of returns to capital are directly reduced. In addition, tax reduction by increasing the rate of economic expansion will tend to raise interest rates and make the country a less attractive place for foreigners to borrow; the outflow of capital will be less than otherwise and perhaps turn around.

Concluding Comment

One objective not mentioned so far may, or may not, overshadow the others. How could one say? In any case it calls for explicit reference, as a reminder to the economists that something outside his immediate sphere may be important: *Good government*. But we can cite high authority. In the words of one of history's greatest economists, Alfred Marshall:

> Government is the most precious of human possessions, and no care can be too great to be spent on enabling it to do its work in the best way: a chief condition to that end is that it should not be set to work for which it is not specially qualified, under the conditions of time and place.

---

[31] As mentioned above, capital taxed abroad contributes to cost of government there rather than here. To the owner the location of any given total of taxes may be a matter of indifference. Nations, however, have high interest in location; and in the world today the physical situation vastly overshadows the source or ownership of funds in deciding the place where profit is taxed.

THE BLEND OF FISCAL AND MONETARY POLICIES FOR THE FUTURE

R. A. MUSGRAVE

THE PROPER blend of fiscal and monetary policy is a subject on which there has been much academic discussion and which of late has been moving into the public spotlight. Unfortunately, our cookbook offers no simple recipe to follow. The proper blend will differ, depending on economic circumstances and on the policy targets that are to be achieved. Moreover, it is not at all clear how the "monetary" and "fiscal" ingredients of the mix should be defined.

As to targets, we wish to achieve economic stability, defined as high employment and full resource utilization without inflation. Also, we wish to achieve an adequate rate of growth of potential output. In either connection, equilibrium in the balance of payments must be considered as well. Beyond this, implications of our mix for fiscal discipline and for the distribution of income should be noted. The proper blend, in each case, hinges on different considerations; and a synthesis, providing the optimal mix for simultaneous achievement of all targets is not easy to come by.

In distinguishing between ingredients, the traditional approach is to think of monetary policy as involving control over the money supply, be it through reserve requirements, open-

155

market operations, or discount rate changes; and of fiscal policy as involving changes in fiscal parameters, i.e., in expenditures or tax yields at a full employment level of income. Thus defined, both policies aim at influencing the overall state of economic ease or restraint. They are both general policies, and this is how the terms are understood in the usual mix discussion. But either policy is open to selective devices as well; and though selective credit controls have lost their popularity in recent years, selective tax devices (such as the investment credit or the interest equalization tax) now have their day. The issue of blend, therefore, is not only one of combining general monetary and fiscal measures. It may be necessary also to add the spices of selective policy, be it of the fiscal or the monetary variety. Also, there is the question of how debt management, that fallen star of yesteryear, should be fitted into the picture.

Stabilization and Growth

We begin with the mix of general policies, designed to achieve the targets of stabilization and growth. Being so closely related, these two targets will be discussed together. The longer-run issue of stable growth is considered first, after which we turn to the shorter-run aspects of dampening cyclical instability.

The problem is to design a blend of fiscal and monetary policy which will secure the desired rate of growth of potential output, and see to it that actual output will move along the potential growth path. The former may be referred to as the "growth" and the latter as the "stabilization" target.

With a given growth rate of the labor force, the growth of potential output is a function of the rate at which the capital stock is increased, and of the rate at which superior techniques are introduced. While the latter rate is not independent of the former, they respond to different policy measures. The blend of general monetary and fiscal policy is related to the rate of capital formation, because it influences the ratio in which private output is divided between consumption and investment. Selective tax and expenditure policies may be used to speed up the rate of technical progress and the rate at which innovations are applied. Our concern here is primarily with the former aspect.

We begin with a highly simplified illustration, designed to show how under certain admittedly unrealistic assumptions, the proper choice of fiscal-monetary mix is uniquely determined. Let us start from a position of high employment and a GNP of, say, $900 billion. Suppose the desired growth or increase in potential output for the next year is set at 5 percent, or $45 billion. If full utilization of labor and capital is to be maintained, the rise in actual output must match the $45 billion rise in potential output. At stable prices, this means that aggregate expenditures must rise by $45 billion. If there is a tendency for expenditures to rise faster, they must be restrained; if the tendency is to lag, they must be expanded. This determines the needed net effect of fiscal and monetary policy on aggregate demand. The degree of restraint which is needed to achieve this net effect—as measured by, say, the level of budget surplus or interest rates—will depend on the buoyancy of the economy at any particular time.

So far, we have determined the net restraint but not the mix, since either policy may be used to restrain or expand total demand. The proper mix is determined by the growth target and the required rate of capital formation. With the given growth in labor force, let us suppose that an addition to the capital stock of $100 billion is required to secure the desired $45 billion growth in potential output.[1] This means that investment must equal $100 billion. Hence $800 billion is left for consumption. Next, we split this total between private and public consumption. Suppose that public consumption requires $125 billion, which level has been set so as to secure efficient resource allocation between public and private needs. This means that private consumption should equal $675 billion. Now we introduce two crucial assumptions: (1) private consumption is related inversely to the level of tax rates but is independent of monetary policy; and (2) investment is related directly to the degree of monetary ease but is independent of

---

[1] To simplify, we assume that the addition to the capital stock is available during the same year in which it is made. In a more sophisticated formulation, lags must be allowed for.

tax rates.[2] In this case, the proper blend is determined unambiguously. Tax rates are to be set at a level where private consumption equals $675 billion, and monetary restraint or ease is to be set at a level where investment equals $100 billion. The argument is then repeated for the next year, when the economy grows from $945 to $992.25 billion and so forth. The matter can be readily translated into a simple model, involving the growth rate, the capital-output ratio, the propensity to consume, and the tax rate, but no purpose is served in pursuing this here.

This simple illustration shows how our double target of stabilization and growth determines the level and mix of stabilization policy. It shows also that a high growth rate requires a policy blend which combines a relatively tight fiscal with a relatively easy monetary policy. The purpose of the former is to hold consumption to a relatively low level by imposing a high tax rate, thereby making room for a relatively high level of investment. The purpose of the latter is to obtain conditions in the credit and capital markets which will secure such investment. This is a proposition which has been advanced repeatedly over the last decade, and which may be found in the Economic Reports of both the late Eisenhower and early Kennedy Administrations.

Before questioning some of the underlying assumptions, let us re-emphasize the distinction between (1) desired net effect on demand, (2) the degree of restraint needed to achieve it, and (3) the appropriate fiscal-monetary policy mix. While (1) and (3) depend on the growth target, (2) depends primarily on the buoyancy of the economy and its response to higher tax rates or monetary restrictions. For any given growth target, the required budget surplus at full employment will be the larger the lower is the propensity to save in the private sector; and the degree of monetary ease will be the higher, the more sluggish is the response of private investment. Similarly, for any given state of buoyancy, the budget surplus will have to be the higher and monetary restraint the lower, the higher is the desired target for growth.

---

[2] To simplify, we assume that all investment is private. This is helpful in the context of our argument, but should not be interpreted as overlooking the important role of public investment.

The preceding argument has considerable appeal because it gives such nice and determinate results. But unfortunately, matters are not this simple. We must now reconsider some of our assumptions, and see how this affects our conclusions on policy mix.

The Fiscal-Monetary Policy Mix

First, consider a situation where investment does not respond sufficiently to monetary ease, be it for reasons of liquidity trap or because the investment schedule is not sufficiently elastic to the cost of funds. This situation, described effectively by the adage that "you can't push a string" may not reoccur in an economy which sets modest growth targets and which maintains the momentum of full employment growth. But suppose it happens. In this case, general policies become inadequate and selective tax devices—such as the investment credit or direct subsidies—may be used to supplement monetary ease. They are essentially similar to the latter in both rate-of-return and availability-of-funds effects. But even this would not help if the investment function is strictly of the accelerator type and responds to neither rate of return nor internal funds. This seems unlikely on the face of it, but most econometric models come close to depicting such a situation. In this case only one growth rate is compatible with stabilization. The issue of mix disappears and fiscal restraint must be adjusted to meet the feasible rate.

Secondly, consider a situation where investment is not independent of the overall level of tax rates but is related inversely thereto. Suppose that the general level of tax rates needed to restrain consumption is so high as to deter investment below the level needed for the growth target. In view of the preferential treatment of capital gains and other features of our tax structure this is unlikely, but suppose that such a situation were to arise.[3] It may then be possible to offset the resulting deterrent to investment by increased monetary ease, in which case general policies remain effective. Where this cannot be done, the general approach becomes again inoperative. Selec-

---

[3] Since tax rates may be raised in so many ways, it is difficult to define what is meant by "general" tax restraint. Suppose we define it as equal across-the-board percentage changes in income tax liabilities.

tive tax measures are needed, involving an investment credit as before, lessened progressively, favorable treatment of capital income, or else an expenditure tax type of approach to deter consumption.

Thirdly, we may reconsider the assumption that monetary policy does not affect consumption. The proposition that higher taxes will deter consumption can hardly be doubted and will stand. The state of the credit market is a major factor in determining the cost and terms of consumer credit as well as of mortgage funds, and has thus a direct bearing on the level of consumption. Moreover, the demand for real balances may also affect consumer behavior. Suppose that credit is eased to permit faster growth through higher investment. Holding more claims, the public may feel it less necessary to save and will spend more. This perverse effect on consumption may be checked with selective credit devices to exclude consumer credit from the increased credit ease. But this is not necessary, as it may be offset (within the framework of general policies) by increased tax restraint.

Also, we must note the mechanical link between fiscal and monetary policy which arises because budget deficits must be financed, and surplus proceeds must be disposed of. This complicates matters but does not disable the "general" policy approach. Increased tax restraint will be linked with monetary ease, depending on what debt retirement is undertaken or what borrowing is dropped. If debt is retired the results will differ, depending on who holds the debt, and on the terms of the debt instrument, such as maturity. To the extent that the credit market is eased, this must be taken into account in the monetary measures. This poses no conflict between the two policy measures, but only establishes an interaction which must be allowed for. Indeed, servicing of deficit or surplus poses only a small part of the debt management issue. The qualitative problem of debt management which, by its nature, is "selective" policy, arises over a much broader front, including the replacement of maturity and were it not for artificial statutory constraints, the exchange of outstanding debt.

All this has assumed that the needed investment will be in the private sector. The issue of mix is changed if public investment is accepted as an alternative. Assuming no change in the required level of total investment, taxes must still be such as to hold down consumption to the same level as before. At the same time, the absolute level of tax rates will have to be higher, since the budget is now enlarged by public capital formation. Nevertheless, the "tightness" of fiscal policy, in the sense of full employment surplus, will be unchanged, since expenditures are increased as well. The required degree of monetary ease will be less, since private investment is now lower. The share of GNP which is purchased privately is reduced and the combined fiscal-monetary restraint is increased.

Finally, we recall the fact that general policy affects growth only via the rate of capital formation. If the flow of innovations can be speeded up as well, a higher rate of growth can be obtained at the given rate of capital formation. This remains true, even if we accept the view that technological progress is embodied in investment. Such is the case because "investment," in this context, includes replacement as well as net investment. Replacement investment is about twice net investment,[4] so that much embodiment can proceed even without rapid expansion of the capital stock. If promotion of technology is relied upon, less investment will thus be needed to reach the growth target. The mix then calls for less budgetary restraint, higher consumption—combined with less monetary ease—and lower investment.

What remains of our original proposition that a general policy mix exists, which will meet the double-target of stability and growth? Leaving aside the matter of innovation, there remains the basic truth that higher growth requires increased investment and reduction in (or smaller increase of) consumption. This means a tighter fiscal policy in the sense of increased budget surplus (or reduced budget deficit) at full employment. Beyond this, one cannot always be certain that the needed level of investment (needed, that is, to secure the growth target) will be forthcoming in response to general monetary policy measures. Chances are that it will, provided a high employment economy is maintained, and the growth target is not too ambitious. If not, general policies may be

---

[4] This applies to nonresident fixed investment by nonfarm, nonfinancial corporations.

supplemented by selective tax incentives to investment. With this qualification, and given the pursuits of these two targets only, general policies should do the job.

The Cyclical Problem and Policy Lags

We now turn to the more difficult matter of short-run stability. Unlike the preceding model, the economy does not behave in a stable and predictable fashion. The mix problem is not solved by deciding on the desired growth rate, "setting" the levels of monetary and fiscal restraints accordingly, and sitting back for the ride. Private expenditure behavior in both the investment and consumption sectors is subject to change, not to speak of public expenditure needs, thereby requiring more or less continuous policy adjustments if the economy is to be maintained on a steady growth path.

The business cycle problem, in its modern version, is not how to level off a smooth sine curve, moving along a horizontal trend in a regular three, four, or seven-year period, as was suggested by traditional cycle theories; nor is it one of overcoming a continuous state of stagnation, with built-in flexibility an undesirable drag, and stabilization policy a one-way road toward expansion. With an expanding economy whose full employment output rises by, say, $40 billion a year, a sustained period of absolute decline in GNP (or only insignificant rise) is unthinkable. The issue, rather, is how to avoid excessive fluctuations in the rate of overall expenditure growth. More specifically, the growth of expenditures should not be permitted to lag behind the growth of potential output so that unemployment will not rise above, say, 4 percent for more than one or two quarters; and it should not be permitted to exceed the potential rate, so that prices do not rise (as the result of "pull" inflation) by more than, say, 1.5 or 2 percent per annum. The policy mix, and the net restraint exercised by fiscal and monetary measures should be designed to accomplish this goal.

Fortunately, the experience of recent years has shown that the path of the economy is fairly stable, and certainly not highly unstable. Unlike the knife-edge model, deviation from the growth path in either direction has not been cumulative, and has been amenable to fiscal and/or monetary control. During the late fifties, failure to undertake appropriate policies left the economy in a highly unsatisfactory position. During the first half of the 1960s, expansionary fiscal policy, first by way of expenditure increase, then by way of tax reduction, succeeded with the support of permissive monetary policy, in pulling the economy up to a reasonably high level of employment. During 1966, pressures towards overexpansion, generated mainly by Vietnam spending and unusually high investment, were contained (if belatedly and unevenly) by monetary restraint. In neither case were the actions perfectly timed or measured, but the results, up to 1965 at least, were satisfactory as compared to earlier periods.

Nevertheless, the need remains to improve our capability to respond quickly and effectively to developing disturbances, be they in the upward or downward direction. In assessing the usefulness of various policy tools for this purpose, we return to the old distinction between (1) the time required to recognize the need for action, (2) the time required to act after recognition of need, and (3) the time which elapses between action and its effectiveness. The first lag need not be considered here. It is, as yet, unfortunately long, but implies equally to both policies and hence is not a matter of mix. Regarding the second lag, monetary policy has traditionally been considered much superior, but recent thinking has improved the rating of fiscal measures.

Regarding the action lag of fiscal policy, traditional emphasis has been on the long time needed to implement public expenditure programs. With the shift in emphasis towards adjustment on the tax side of the budget, this consideration carries less weight. Given the nature of the modern income tax and its withholding system, across-the-board changes in tax rates can be implemented very quickly, indeed in a matter of weeks. The problem, rather, is how long it takes to secure legislative action on such a move. To reduce this part of the time lag, various proposals have been advanced to delegate authority to the executive, as recommended by the Commission on Money and Credit and proposed by the President in 1964, though, partly in response to congressional reaction, for rate reduction only. These proposals seem as yet politically impracticable, and other less radical arrangements have been suggested. These involve advance legislation by Congress, subject only to joint resolution in response to a presidential request to be made when action is needed. One of the crucial points, in any of these plans, is to devise means by which the broader structural issues of tax reform can be separated from cyclical adjustments in tax rates, and the latter can be made in a simple and distributionally neutral form.

Some people take a more complacent view and argue that there is no need for such arrangements since Congress will act promptly when called upon. I do not share this optimism. There is good reason to surmise that the administration's failure to act in late 1965 or early 1966 reflected in part at least the Congress' unwillingness to respond. But quite apart from this, a routine mechanism for administrative action, and responsibility for using it, would be most helpful in securing such action, as well as in providing a setting in which stabilizing tax changes, like open-market operations, come to be accepted as a matter of course. As suggested by the nature of the 1964 proposal for delegation, as well as the experience of 1965/66, politics interferes with restraining, if not easing, tax action, and there is urgent need for improving this situation.

Turning now to the effectiveness lag, the advantage is on the fiscal rather than on the monetary side. Changes in the level of government orders are reflected fairly promptly in changes in demand; and even changes in the level of transfer payments or income tax withholding will be reflected in the level of consumption expenditures largely, according to the 1964-65 experience, within a period of two quarters. Response to monetary measures depends primarily on investment. Hence it takes longer to become effective, and lingers on for a longer period.

Time elapses before changes in open-market policy are reflected in the money market, and before changes in the mortgage market come to be reflected in expenditure changes. The latter lag is not so long in the case of housing starts, but it is considerable for fixed capital investment by business. Such investment plans are made well in advance, and changes in the availability or cost of funds, be it because of monetary measures or changes in the investment credit are likely to have little effect for six months or more. Inventory investment can respond more quickly, but the cost of funds is not a major factor if price expectations are bullish. In all, the restrictive monetary measures initiated in the fall of 1965 and accentuated in the spring of 1966 are just now reaching their full effect, and it will take some time for a reversal of policy to become felt. The countercyclical effectiveness of monetary policy—especially with regard to plant and equipment investment—is thus greatly reduced by a lag factor, especially where short cycles are concerned. At the same time, this does not interfere with its usefulness for the longer-run purposes of growth policy.

While empirical knowledge on policy lags is still very unsatisfactory, we seem to be left with the unhappy conclusion that tax policy has a longer action lag, especially in the direction of restraint, while monetary policy has the longer effectiveness lag. If the former is to be reduced in the future, this will involve not only administrative or legislative arrangements which permit quicker action, but also economic education that will make it politically profitable or at least possible for an administration to recommend action when needed.

A further consideration entering into the mix of countercyclical action is the structural impact of various measures. An across-the-board change in income tax rates acts primarily upon consumption expenditures of all kinds. This generates subsequent changes in investment, but the initial impact is on consumption. A change in credit conditions acts primarily— at least in the short run as shown by the experience of 1965/66 —upon the mortgage market and residential construction. State-local construction also tends to be a primary point of impact. While the effect of both restraints comes to be generalized in the "second round" of response, the initial impact differs.

There is much to be said for aiming restrictive or expansionary measures directly at that sector of the economy in which the instability originates. If the center of instability is in plant and equipment expenditures as was the case in the boom of 1957, and apart from the inopportune rise in defense spending, also in 1965-66, there is a case for directing stabilizing measures at such outlays. Unfortunately, both our general policy measures fail this test. The most effective approach is through selective tax devices such as countercyclical adjustments in the investment credit, turning it from a credit to a tax if needed, or in investment reserves of the Swedish type. While this is subject to much the same effectiveness lag as general monetary measures, it is superior as far as precision of impact point is concerned. Whereas monetary restriction acts primarily on housing, adjustments in the credit device deal with plant and equipment as well. Moreover, use of the credit device bypasses the dangers of "financial panic" which arose at the height of the tightening operation last year and which would have precluded further tightening even if economic conditions should have called for it. The proper countercyclical mix, especially over longer swings, will therefore be one which combines appropriate selective tax devices with general fiscal and monetary restraints, rather than one which combines general policies only.

Fiscal Restraint and Inflation

There are various reasons why it is desirable to focus the restraining and expansionary impact at the source of instability. For one thing, instability feeds upon itself and requires increasingly strong stabilizing measures. For another, the very purpose of stabilizing action on the restrictive side is to forestall inflation with a minimum of underutilization and unemployment. If the impact of restriction is centered in the housing market, as has now been the case, the general reduction in demand which follows in the "second round" is purchased at the cost of excess capacity and perhaps unemployment in that sector. This may well have been preferable to a policy of no restraint with inflation, but inferior to a more generalized expenditure restraint, especially if supplemented by restrictive action in the plant and equipment sector, where overexpansion originated in both 1957 and 1966.

An additional case for appropriate balance between fiscal and monetary restraints arises from the need for coordinating cyclical stabilization with growth policy. If the latter requires that investment on the average comprise a certain fraction of GNP, successive levels of investment which result from short-run adjustment must average out to meet this constraint. Again there is much to be said for holding the rate of investment at the desired level, thus securing a steady growth of potential (as well as actual) output. If, on the contrary, potential output is permitted to grow in spurts, the coordination of actual output growth will be that much more difficult.

Whatever the proper policy mix in short-run stabilization, general fiscal and monetary measures, including selective ones, do not suffice to assure that high employment will coexist with price level stability. General policies can secure an appropriate division of output between consumption and capital formation, and an appropriate rate of total expenditure growth. They can be adjusted to avoid "pull" inflation or deflation, but other factors enter in determining how high a level of employment can be sustained without inflation. Two aspects of the problem should be distinguished, both of which enter into the shape of the Phillips curve, or relation between price rise and level of employment.

First, there is the troublesome but manageable task of fitting labor supply to labor demand. This is a problem which would arise even in a highly competitive labor market. As the economy proceeds from a high to a low level of unemployment— consider the experience from 1960 to 1966—previously unemployed resources are put to work. Growth of output due to growth of labor force and productivity is temporarily supplemented by gains from increased utilization. But sooner or later this absorption becomes more difficult. Bottlenecks arise and further increase in output involves price rise caused by shortages. Thus, the large output gains with little or no price rise from 1961 to 1965 were then followed by emerging shortages and price increase. This development reflected the higher level of utilization which was reached, as well as the rate of expenditure increase. Up to mid-1965 the rise of output was not excessive, notwithstanding frequent warnings to the contrary, but thereafter it came to be. Partly this was due to the rising rate of expenditure growth, as adaptability of the labor market is a function of time as well as the level of employment. Adaptability may be aided in the longer run through labor market policies including training and retraining, increased mobility, and so forth. If this is done, it should be possible in time to reduce unemployment further without increase in bottlenecks. These are important aspects of public policy for high employment, but they are outside the fiscal-monetary sphere.

Second, there is the more difficult question of responsible wage-price behavior in a high employment economy, where both labor and product market are subject to administered pricing policies. Suppose that the security given by a past record and future promise of high employment results in wage demands in excess of productivity gains; and that the employers are willing to accept and pass on such wage increases to the consumer. Moreover, suppose that firms, operating in a seller's market, add to upward price pressures through pricing policies of their own. Monetary-fiscal policy may then choose between disciplining the market by refusing to expand demand thereby causing unemployment, or sanctioning inflation by permitting the level of expenditures to rise. Achieving both targets is now outside the reach of fiscal-monetary policy. The problem, rather, is one of making market behavior comply with a set of rules such as expressed in the Council's wage-price guideposts, be it through moral suasion or stronger means of incomes policy. While it is my belief that some such measures may well prove necessary, and, if so, will be worth the gain, to secure price stability, this is a problem which cannot be dealt with in the context of this paper.

The mix between monetary and fiscal policy in cyclical stabilization has to be made on various grounds. With regard to flexibility, monetary policy has the advantage of a shorter action lag, while tax measures seem to enjoy a shorter effectiveness lag. With regard to structural impact, neither type of general policy is effective in securing prompt response in plant and equipment outlays, but general tax measures tend to be more balanced in their impact than general monetary measures; and selective tax devices (such as the investment credit) permit concentration of policy impact on business investment. With regard to coordination of short-run stability with long-run growth, coordination of both policy devices is needed. In all, there is no neat prescription for the proper policy blend. The mix of general policies has to be adjusted as economic conditions change over the cycle, and there is much to be said for supplementing it by selective tax devices. However this may be, the monetary-fiscal mix is but a part, and probably the easier part, of the problem. Responsible wage-price behavior is needed as well, but is not within the realm of this discussion.

Balance-of-Payments Objectives

We now turn to certain other policy targets for which the fiscal-monetary mix is of considerable importance. These include equilibrium in the balance of payments, the achievement of fiscal discipline, and equity in the distributive effects of stabilization policy.

Stabilization policy bears on the balance of payments on both trade and capital account. Effects on trade account result from changes in both prices and output. Inflationary price rise is equivalent to appreciation and tends to worsen the account. Increase in output due to higher employment in turn is likely to increase imports more than exports, so that a high employment policy on balance tends to be unfavorable on trade account. But growth due to productivity gains is a different matter, and may well improve the trade account. To the extent that a higher rate of capital formation expedites the introduction of technology, a policy mix favorable to growth may thus be favorable on trade account.

However this may be, the shorter-run significance of policy blend relates primarily to the capital rather than the trade account. High employment is now favorable in its effect on long-term capital flows, as the attractiveness of domestic investment is increased. Moreover, capital movements, and those of short-term capital in particular, respond to interest rate differentials. To the extent that monetary restraint comes to be reflected in higher interest rates, this tends to reduce capital outflow and/or attract capital inflow, and the opposite holds for the case of monetary ease. A policy mix of tight money and easy fiscal policy is more favorable to short-term capital flows but less so to growth, and vice versa.[5]

---

[5] This discussion refers to a regime of fixed exchange rates. Monetary restraint and ease is effective in reducing or expanding domestic demand, as well as reducing or expanding net capital outflow.

If exchange rates were flexible, equilibrium in the balance of payments would be maintained automatically. Assuming perfect capital mobility, short-term rates would be equalized at home and abroad. Monetary policy, in this case, would not be effective in controlling domestic demand via changes in interest rates. Monetary restraint (by potentially inducing capital inflow) would bring about appreciation of the exchange rate and reduce the surplus (increase the deficit) on trade account, thus giving rise to a restrictive income effect on the domestic economy. The reverse would apply for increased monetary ease.

This has been a significant factor in U.S. policy during the 1960s. Up to mid-1965 the policy need was for expansion, in order to close the gap between potential and actual output. The brunt of this expansionary action was carried by the fiscal side, with monetary policy moving along on a more or less permissive basis. This was in line with the needs of the balance-of-payments situation. The substantial decline in interest rates which would have been needed to close the gap via monetary expansion, if at all possible, would have greatly worsened the already serious balance-of-payments deficit on capital account. Indeed, the United States repeatedly but unsuccessfully pleaded for increased reliance on fiscal rather than monetary restraint by European countries, so as to permit it to reach high employment while protecting its balance of payments.

After a high level of employment had been reached in mid-1965, a further rise in expenditures for Vietnam, coincident with an investment boom, called for restrictive moves. These took the form of monetary rather than tax restriction. From mid-1965 to mid-1966, short-term interest rates rose from 4 to 5.5 percent, while bond yields increased from 3.6 to 4.5 percent. In addition, the interest equalization tax was in effect. Over the same period, exchange losses from direct foreign investment increased sharply, it being apparent that restrictive monetary policy had little or no effect on this respect. Long-term foreign capital inflow rose somewhat, perhaps as the result of generally higher yields in the U.S. At the same time, there was little change with regard to U.S. short-term capital outflow. This is explainable since foreign rates rose as well. If we assume that the latter would have occurred anyhow, the tightening of U.S. rates may thus have prevented further outflow and have been more effective than appears at first sight.

Turning to future policy, the administration's case is now for a change in mix, combining fiscal tightening with monetary relaxation, holding constant the level of overall restraint; or for primarily monetary easing if a net relaxation of restraint is called for. This will help prospective homeowners and the construction industry, but it may well be detrimental with regard to short-term capital flow. The conflict may be reduced to some degree by various types of selective action. Debt management may again aim at holding short rates high while permitting long rates to fall, an approach which previously was attempted with modest vigor in the so-called "operation twist." Also, it may be possible through government lending policies to relieve the mortgage market. Other possibilities are to attract foreign—especially central banks—funds by premium interest rates, or to apply selective measures to check domestic capital outflow. These range from a stepped up interest equalization tax as now proposed, to neutralizing the tax treatment of foreign investment income, or even the imposition of penalizing tax measures.

In all, it appears that the choice of general policy mix may well be incapable of achieving the domestic as well as balance-of-payments targets. A potential conflict is present with regard to both high employment and growth objectives. At the same time, selective controls can be constructed to deal with the situation, and given the relatively small size of the foreign sector in the U.S. economy, it should indeed be possible to overcome this difficulty.

Fiscal Discipline

As balance-of-payments considerations limit the freedom of monetary policy, so may considerations of "fiscal discipline" limit that of fiscal policy. But while the former conflict arises from the nature of economic responses, the latter is essentially a political issue.

Suppose for a moment that there were no problems of "fiscal politics" and that the level of public expenditures and taxes was determined upon an efficient basis. We would then be confronted with a two-step policy determination. First, it would be decided what share of total resources should be devoted to public purposes, or what share of potential, high employment income should be devoted to the satisfaction of public wants. Secondly, it would be decided what level of taxation was needed to secure the proper level of aggregate demand, given (1) this level of public expenditures, and (2) the fiscal-monetary mix as set by the growth target. Depending on the underlying economic conditions, this may call for a deficit or surplus at full employment; but whatever may be needed, there would be no conflict between providing for the proper level of public services, securing full resource utilization, and achieving the desired growth target.

But this may not be the case if we drop the assumption of efficient policy determination. Behavior may and, indeed, tends to be such that the true "cost" of public services, the opportunity cost of resource use for public rather than private purposes, is understated in periods of deficit and overstated in periods of surplus. As a result, public expenditures tend to be too high, relative to their opportunity costs, in deficit, and too low in surplus periods. Looking at the matter in terms of policy change, need for expansionary action may lead to unjustified expenditure increase, rather than tax reduction, as exemplified by the ditch-digging approach to depression spending; and the need for restrictive action may lead to unjustified expenditure cutback, as exemplified by the even more distressing example of prospective cutbacks in the poverty program.

Now it might be argued that the longer-run need of stabilization will be basically for expansion, and that a variety of other factors cause the general level of public services to be too low rather than too high. I share these views, but cannot follow the conclusion that this justifies any upward pressure on expenditure no matter what the reason may be. Securing a proper balance of resource use between the public and the private sector should be a matter of public education, and not be left to the chance that cyclical conditions will support the proper bias. Expansionary effects of fiscal policy can be induced by tax reduction as well as expenditure increase, and the two, resource use and stabilization, decisions should be made on their respective grounds.

A radical support of "discipline" might suggest that the budget should be balanced,[6] while stabilization is secured through monetary policy. But this is totally unacceptable. Monetary policy alone will not be able to secure both high employment and the desired growth rate. And even if only the former target is considered, drastic fluctuations in credit conditions over the cycle might well have untenable structural implications for the economy, such as violent fluctuations in housing. The question, rather, is whether a midway solution

---

[6] We note in passing that the budget balance which is relevant for purposes of the discipline argument is not necesarily the same which is relevant with regard to stabilization.

can be secured. A first approach to the problem, popular in the postwar years, was that the budget should be balanced over the cycle. With the revamping of fiscal economics in terms of growth, this is now restated as the rule that the budget should be balanced at a level of full employment income. This would avoid fiscal drag,[7] while permitting the forces of built-in flexibility to produce a deficit in periods of lagging expenditure growth, and a surplus in periods of overexpansion. Before evaluating this rule, note that its implementation is not equivalent to a hands-off policy but requires action. After balance at full employment is established, the rule is that any expenditure change should be matched by a tax yield change. If the expenditure increase exceeds the built-in gain in yield, a tax increase would be called for. Assuming expenditures to be constant or to grow less, the policy would call for annual tax rate reductions, so as to offset the built-in revenue gain which results as potential output rises.

This latest version of fiscal orthodoxy has appeal, but is nevertheless unacceptable on both secular and cyclical grounds. Regarding the longer-run view, there is no assurance that the growth of actual and desired potential output can be synchronized while maintaining a budget with potential balance at full employment. While the economic record of the 1960s has been good, the high capacity performance has been associated with a substantial and repeated injection of fiscal leverage. The elimination of "fiscal drag" from 1961 to 1965 reduced the full-employment surplus by about $15 billion. Moreover, it was associated with a $30 billion rise, 1960-65, in the absolute level of the budget. The general pattern was thus one of sustained fiscal expansion. In spite of this, the outlook for the economy is not one of unmitigated strength. Indeed, it seems rather unlikely that the high employment record will be continued over the next decade, if henceforth a neutral fiscal policy—maintaining balance at full employment—is pursued. Such is the case especially in view of the balance-of-payments constraint on easy money, but may remain so even if a higher degree of monetary freedom is restored. The rule might thus have to be amended, calling for modest deficits at full employment.

---

[7] Fiscal drag is defined as an automatic increase in budget surplus at full employment which results if the built-in increase in tax yield is not offset by an equal increase in expenditures.

This would still meet the major needs of fiscal discipline, as budget balancing would apply at the margin, though not for the total budget. There remains, however, the question whether any such rule, even if amended to meet secular needs, would leave sufficient flexibility to deal with short-run fluctuations. While the power of built-in flexibility has risen with the ratio of budget to GNP, I do not believe that it is sufficient. Active use of fiscal policy, adjustments in the state of budgetary balance at full employment, cannot be dispensed with on cyclical grounds. Excessive reliance on monetary measures soon runs into limitations, witness 1966, and has serious structural effects. The support of tax adjustments is needed. The problem of fiscal discipline cannot be denied, nor can it be solved at the cost of disqualifying the fiscal tool for cyclical use. Other approaches to the discipline problem, pertaining to budgetary procedure and to the mechanism of tax and expenditure legislation, need to be found.

Income Distribution

Finally, the impact of the fiscal-monetary policy mix on income distribution needs to be allowed for. Traditionally, the design of tax legislation has always been considered in relation to income distribution. When tax changes are made, a good deal of attention is given to whose burden is raised or lowered. The question of progression is debated, matters of equity are examined, and tax policy is recognized as a tool by which income distribution can be adjusted. The current debate over the negative income tax is but a new chapter in this old and proper tradition.

But strangely enough, similar issues are rarely raised with regard to monetary policy. Monetary authorities like to think of their tool as being neutral, adjusted in response to impersonal market forces, and in accordance with objectively definable needs of price level stability and more lately, high employment. "Leaning against the wind," or responding to "return to normal credit conditions" reflects this spirit. Yet, it is evident that credit restraint or ease, is an alternative to fiscal restraint or ease.

Taking the case of restraint, let us suppose that the tax restraint is in the form of an equal percentage increase in income tax liabilities across the board. What are the distributional differences between this form of restraint, and that exercised by an equivalent of tightening credit conditions? Viewed in this way, the concept of "differential incidence"—which, in fact, is the only workable incidence concept—applies to a comparison between equivalent monetary and tax restraints, just as it applies to one between alternative tax restraints.

We cannot take the time here to pursue this matter in detail. Instead, we shall advance the hypothesis, which I believe would be borne out by careful investigation, that substitution of general credit restraint for tax restraint would be regressive, that it would redistribute income from the lower to the higher income groups; and that substitution of such tax easing for credit easing would be progressive. Similar considerations apply to a change in mix, leaving net economic restraint unchanged. A substitution of tax for credit restraint would be progressive, while the reverse substitution would be regressive. A general policy mix favorable to high growth (easy money and tight budget) thus tends to be on the progressive side.

This conclusion is based on the distributive effects of changes in the level of interest and income tax rates. It is strengthened by the fact that the rationing aspects of credit tightening, apart from changes in interest cost, are more burdensome to low income consumers who are not in a position to finance their own consumer credit. On the other hand, it may have to be qualified if in order to secure high investment, the tax structure has to be rendered less progressive, so that "general" tax changes do in fact assume a selective flavor.[8]

Blend of General and Selective Measures

We must now gather the threads and see what conclusions can be drawn if all the targets are considered. We assume first that the mix is to be comprised of general monetary and fiscal measures only. Thereafter, selective monetary and tax de-

---

[8] These conclusions might be changed if a different type of "general" tax change is stipulated, say, variations in sales tax, or in the first bracket rate of the income tax. In this sense our conclusion is somewhat arbitrary. Yet, there is a general tendency for this distributional hypothesis to hold. It explains in some measure the politics of fiscal *vs.* credit adjustment and is not without significance in the determination of the policy mix.

vices are allowed for. Our conclusions with regard to the various policy targets are as follows:

1. We begin with the longer-run aspects of stability and growth. Both general policy tools are effective in adjusting the overall level of demand or secular rate of expenditure growth. Such is the case, at least, if we assume the economy to continue in a generally strong position. This leaves us free to use the monetary tool so as to set capital formation at the rate needed by the growth target and to use tax policy to secure the appropriate level of consumption and total demand.

2. Achieving short-run stability depends heavily upon the flexibility with which policy tools may be used and the rate at which they become effective. Monetary policy is superior in some respects and tax policy in others. To avoid structural distortions and to permit the maintenance of a fairly steady growth path of potential output, adjustment in both policy tools will be needed. Even then, it may be difficult to reconcile stability and growth objectives, especially since monetary measures do not provide an effective short-run control over plant and equipment expenditure of business.

3. The effectiveness of the general policy mix is greatly diminished by balance-of-payments constraints. If monetary policy, via effects of interest rates on capital flow, is to be used to restore equilibrium in the balance of payments, the same tool cannot also be used to control the rate of growth of potential output. The larger the payments deficit that is to be closed, the higher will interest rates and hence the lower will the growth rate of potential output have to be, and vice versa. Whatever the decision, fiscal policy may be used to secure stabilization, but either determination of the growth target or balance-of-payments control must be sacrificed in setting monetary policy.

4. A particular mix of general policy—including changes in reserve position and across-the-board changes in income tax rates—may have undesirable distributional implications. Yet, a change in mix, undertaken for distributional reasons may interfere with the growth and stabilization targets.

5. The fiscal-discipline objective imposes further demands on the fiscal-monetary mix, from both the secular and cyclical point of view. If fiscal discipline considerations were permitted to determine the state of budgetary balance, only monetary

policy would remain to deal with the other targets. This it cannot do. Even if balance-of-payments and distributional aspects are overlooked, monetary policy alone cannot deal with both stabilization and growth. If stabilization (the proper level of total expenditures) is given priority, the rate of investment and growth, will have to be the accommodating factor. If the balance-of-payments purpose is to be served, as well, the situation becomes even worse. Monetary policy must now serve three masters, whereas it can only please one.

In conclusion, there is little reason to expect that a satisfactory achievement of all targets can be had by securing the proper blend of general fiscal and monetary measures. While this blend is important, it is only a part of the larger policy problem. This finding is neither novel nor disturbing. We do not have to think very hard to come up with a set of selective policy measures which, in conjunction with the proper general mix, will bring all or at least most targets within reach.

Consider first the possible conflicts between stabilization, growth, and the balance of payments. Retaining general tax policy to set the proper level of consumption, the situation may be resolved by freeing the interest rate to equilibrate the balance of payments, while applying other devices to control the rate of investment. For this, a variety of tax measures are available, be they positive or negative investment credits, initial allowances, accelerated depreciation, and so forth. Indeed, such measures may well offer more effective control over the rate of private capital formation, which is of major relevance to growth, than do variations in monetary ease. Or, the problem may be resolved by using general monetary policy to control investment, while using other instruments to influence capital flows. In this case, the previously noted approaches to capital flow—interest equalization tax, revised tax treatment of foreign investment income, differential interest rates—come into play.

Turning to the distributional implications of the general policy mix, we again may use other policies to resolve potential conflicts. If the mix is too "regressive," this may be corrected simply by offsetting changes in the tax structure making for increased progression. The situation may be more difficult, however, if it appears that high investment requires high rates of return. Since capital income is distributed much more unequally than work income, a high investment target might thus impose a check to progressive taxation. In fact, capital gains treatment already results in a regressive effective income tax rate at the upper end of the income scale, so that this concern is rather removed from reality. Moreover, the difficulty might be resolved to some extent by concentrating investment incentives on low-income investors, along the lines of the dividend deduction.

Concluding Observations

In concluding, let me add two observations. First, economic theory can help us to determine whether available policy instruments are adequate to reach a desired target, or which additional tools may be needed to solve the problem. But solving the numbers game of equating tools and targets is a far cry from achieving a successful policy result in their application. To show that everything can be done, if only it is done right, is a useful seminar exercise, but not a sufficient prescription for so doing. The uncertainty of economic change and the difficulty of predicting lags as well as magnitudes in the responses to various policies, make it exceedingly difficult to accomplish a set of interacting objectives. While much has been learned in recent decades and much success has been achieved in recent years, we still have a long way to go before balanced growth can be operated in a smooth fashion, or before a simple prescription can be given regarding the proper mix. Such is the case quite apart from the fact that the most difficult question—most difficult, that is, in political rather than economic terms—is not a matter of fiscal or monetary policy, but of securing social discipline in the conduct of wage and price determination at high employment. The "new" economics has taught us how to reach and maintain high employment. The "newer" economics or politics of maintaining stability at full employment remains to be written.

Secondly, since we have some way to go before all targets can be achieved at once, it is only prudent to establish a priority among targets and, where needed, to define acceptable trade-off ratios. As far as I am concerned, high employment needs to be given priority over higher growth of potential output, and balance-of-payments considerations should be approached by direct controls if needed, rather than be permitted to interfere seriously with the general fiscal-policy mix needed to achieve these prime targets. My ranking is based on the fact that high employment, above all, is needed to overcome racial bias and poverty, it being evident that the marginal incidence of increased unemployment has devastating effects in this respect. Since I consider these to pose our major domestic policy issues, I cannot give on high employment. As to the possibility of reconciling price level stability with high employment, the issue is not one of monetary-fiscal mix. It arises, no matter how the high employment is reached, and the question is whether it can be resolved with moral suasion, or whether a more forceful participation of public policy in the process of wage-price determination will be needed. To me, the latter course is to be preferred, if it appears that the alternatives are considerable unemployment or sustained, if slow, inflation. Again, the answer lies in combining appropriate selective measures with the general mix, if in fact, it appears that general measures alone cannot do the job.

DISCUSSION AND COMMENTS ON PAPERS BY PROFESSOR HARRISS AND PROFESSOR MUSGRAVE

Professor Gottfried Haberler

The two very excellent papers to which we have just listened covered a lot of ground, and I can therefore touch only on the problems which have been raised. I shall discuss primarily Professor Musgrave's paper because it was the first one which I received; moreover, there is perhaps less to disagree with in the paper by Professor Harriss. Both speakers talk of targets and instruments. Let me address myself to four targets only: growth, employment, price stability, and equilibrium in the balance of payments. Of course, I need not say, after the excellent discussion by Professor Harriss, that none of these targets is really an end in itself. They are a means to an end and they are not undifferentiated homogeneous targets but complexes of objectives or targets, each with slightly divergent versions and facets. For brevity's sake I shall, however, ignore such refinements.

It was perhaps not sufficiently stressed in the papers that there frequently arise conflicts between the different targets. Usually, it is not possible to aim at all four targets at the same time without violating some of them. There is, first of all, the familiar conflict between, on the one hand, growth and employment and, on the other hand, price stability; similarly, there is often a conflict between the first two targets, growth and employment, and the balance of payments. If you have a wage push, you cannot have a very high level of employment without having rising costs and prices and without getting into balance-of-payments difficulties.

Furthermore, there is sometimes a conflict which is not so often mentioned, between the target of rapid long-run growth and the objective of a very high level of employment. This conflict can arise at different levels of employment for two reasons. First at a certain level of employment, with modern aggressive labor unions, wage push becomes strong. This leads to inflation which sooner or later becomes intolerable. Since "incomes policies" and "guideposts for non-inflationary wage behavior" do not work or work only for a short while, inflation will have to be stopped eventually by monetary and/or fiscal policies. This clearly is not good for growth or employment. At what level of employment (or unemployment) this happens depends on the power and aggressiveness of labor unions. But, secondly, even if there were no unions and higher levels of employment could be reached without creating intolerable inflation, a deeper conflict between growth and inflation appears: a fully or almost fully-employed economy becomes brittle and inflexible. This again is not good for growth.

Summarizing, one could say that occasional lapses from full employment are necessary to check inflation and to keep the economy flexible. In other words, driving the economy at "high pressure" for a long time at continuously very high levels of employment will not guarantee maximum long-run growth. How much slack for how long and how often would be best calculated to maximize long-run growth, is an extremely difficult question to which I do not dare to give even a tentative answer in the short time at my disposal. Let me only express the wish that economists would face this problem squarely and recognize that there is a problem. All too often it is entirely ignored.

Now let me comment on some of Professor Musgrave's arguments. He begins with a "simple model" which he calls "admittedly unrealistic." It surely is unrealistic, perhaps even more so than he suggests. In due course he qualifies the heroic simplifications and the meat of his discussion is really in the qualification. He reaches the well-known conclusion that for rapid growth a tight fiscal policy and easy money policy would be the ideal combination, because a tight budget keeps consumption down and easy money (a low interest rate) stimulates investment. That is correct provided the right kind of taxes are used, namely, taxes that fall primarily on consumption, such as the basic income tax or indirect taxes. Still better would be to tighten the budget by reducing unproductive government expenditures for which there is plenty of scope. A tight budget brought about by highly progressive taxes which reduce profits, check enterprise, and discourage investment would do no good in stimulating growth. Unfortunately, that is a program which has much political appeal.

When he comes to the problem of "cyclical stability," Professor Musgrave distinguishes between what he calls the "modern version" of the business cycle problem from "the traditional cycle theories." The older writers thought in terms of "leveling off a smooth sine curve" while now "the issue is rather how to avoid excessive fluctuations in expenditure growth." I am not prepared to accept this sharp distinction between the old and the new economics of the business cycle. On a certain level of abstraction even the most modern cycle theorists speak in terms of smooth sine curves and some of the "older" writers, for example, the masters of the National Bureau of Economic Research, emphatically rejected the notion that sine curves are an adequate representation of business cycles. Nor can I accept the view that is now often expressed and which Musgrave may have alluded to, although he does not say so explicitly, that the older business cycle theorists taught that business cycle policy should aim at steering the economy on a "path through cyclical midpoints," that is, on a level with considerable slack and unemployment.[1] I do not know of any "older" writer who has put forward that view.

Professor Musgrave is critical of the anti-inflationist measures of the Eisenhower Administration in the late 1950s which "left the economy in a highly unsatisfactory condition." Professor McCracken, who was in the midst of things at the time, admitted in his excellent speech this morning that mistakes were made. That surely is true, but the critics should not for-

---

[1] This is Professor J. Tobin's formulation, *The Intellectual Revolution in U.S. Economic Policy Making* (London: 1966).

get two things. First, the U.S. balance of payments was in very bad shape in 1959. It was the only year during the post-war period in which there was no surplus on goods and services. As a consequence of the drastic anti-inflationary measures of the Eisenhower Administration, the surplus on goods and services rose from nil in 1959 to $4 billion in 1960 and on to $8.4 billion in 1964. Since then it has again declined to $5.3 million in 1966. Secondly, the anti-inflationary measures did create unemployment, 5.6 percent in 1960. In 1964, it was still 5.2 percent, and it was only at the end of 1965 that unemployment declined to 4 percent. Without the drastic anti-inflationary measures of 1959, the long Kennedy-Johnson prosperity would have immediately run into inflationary difficulties, instead of only four years later and the expansion probably could not have been kept going for so long.[2]

Since 1965 inflation has again become a serious problem. As Professor Musgrave says "pressures towards overexpansion generated mainly by Vietnam spending were contained, if belatedly and unevenly, by monetary restraints" in 1966. A few comments would seem to be in order. First, we should recall that nondefense expenditures, too, have grown by leaps and bounds during the last 2½ years. Second, as Professor Musgrave points out, the anti-inflationary restraint was left to monetary policy. Fiscal policy was not used and when the first moves were made by the Fed to use monetary restraints against inflation by raising the discount rate in December, 1965, the answer was a storm of criticism on the part of the administration from the President down, and in Congress. Monetary policy has become much more a football of politics than it used to be. Partly, no doubt, as a consequence of that fact, it has been somewhat jerky during the last two years. After the row about the rise in the discount rate in December, 1965, the Fed leaned over backwards and continued expanding money supply at an annual rate of 6 percent until April, 1966. When inflation continued and accelerated, it belatedly stepped hard on the brake in April or May. This resulted in an abrupt decline of the rate of growth of money supply from 6 percent until April, 1966, to about zero from May to October or No-

---

[2] For further details I refer to my pamphlet, *Inflation: Its Causes and Cures*. Revised and enlarged edition with A New Look at Inflation (Washington, D.C.: American Enterprise Institute, 1966).

vember. Since then money supply has been again expanding at a substantial rate.

These abrupt changes have been widely criticized—rightly, I believe. I myself would not go so far as to propose an iron-clad rule that money supply should be raised by a fixed percentage a year, 3 to 4 percent is the figure usually mentioned. But a somewhat more flexible and gentler operation of the monetary brake than we witnessed since 1966 would certainly be desirable. It should also be recalled that during the expansion years of fairly stable prices, money supply rose more gradually and at a lower rate than since 1965.

These recent episodes shed a good deal of light on the problem of blending monetary and fiscal policies. Professor Musgrave advocates more frequent across-the-board changes in tax rates. He realizes that this would require congressional delegation of authority to make such changes to the executive. He also favors "selective tax devices such as countercyclical adjustments in the investment credit, turning it from a credit to a tax if needed." To take up the last proposal first, it would seem to me that the investment credit device is especially unsuited for frequent changes. I was impressed by Father Hogan's paper yesterday which showed that the short-run effects of the suspension of the investment credit in September, 1966, were very small. It is generally agreed, I believe, that this suspension was a mistake and despite official disclaimer the reinstatement this year shows that the administration realized its mistake.

This highlights the difficulties or rather impossibility of "fine tuning" of the economy by fiscal policy measures. The investment tax device is, to repeat, an especially unsuited instrument for that purpose. The objections to changing the basic income tax rates, if it were politically feasible, may be less weighty. But it is probably not possible administratively to change tax rates every half year. And suppose the administration had had authority to change tax rates: Would it have used it in 1965 or early 1966? The evidence suggests that it would not have used it in time.

There seems to emerge a consensus that if there is to be "fine tuning" of the economy, it has to be done by monetary policy. Mr. Ackley, too, has expressed this view in a recent speech. There is, however, the Friedman-Brunner-Meltzer School which denies that fine tuning can be achieved by monetary policy because of the long and variable lags with which monetary policy measures operate. I myself, to repeat, am not ready to accept a binding rule for monetary policy to increase the supply of money by a fixed percentage and to refrain from any deviation from that norm. We simply don't know enough about those lags to make it prudent to bind our hands. But agreement may be possible that monetary policy could and should be operated in a less jerky fashion than it was during the last three years.

One last remark on this matter. Different people who use the words "fine tuning" have probably different notions of the degree of fineness. In a sense, the whole period since the Second World War was concerned with fine tuning. Comparing the 22 years which have elapsed since the end of that war with the 22 years after the end of the First World War, one cannot help being struck by the tremendous improvement. The two decades after 1918 saw two deep depressions, 1920-21 and the catastrophic depression of the 1930s. Nothing of that sort has visited the United States or the world at large since 1945. Moreover, there is fairly general agreement that the improvement is not fortuitous or temporary, that on the contrary we really know how to prevent deep depressions. However, disagreement persists on the question how much can we improve the record of the postwar period, which is, to repeat, quite impressive by prewar standards? My tentative answer is: Somewhat but not very much. If we tried to suppress the mild cycles which we have experienced since 1945 altogether, we could do it only by paying a high price in terms of inflation and progressive regimentation of the economy. This development would not only be obnoxious in itself, but would also result in slower long-run growth of the economy.

Let me add a word on the balance of payments. Professor Musgrave expresses the view that a "high employment" policy may be favorable for the balance of payments because it makes investment attractive and this tends to prevent capital exports or even induces capital imports. This theory was very popular in the early 1960s, but it proved to be a great miscalculation. True, the economy did expand, profits rose, and investment was stimulated. But capital exports soared at the same time instead of declining. The British had the same disappointment. The Conservative government, a year before the election which brought the Labor party to power, tried to carry out a "flight forward" from its balance-of-payments miseries. They engaged in bold monetary expansion and hoped that better profit expectations would improve the capital balance and maybe even the trade balance would be favorably affected by a larger volume of production. The result was a colossal external deficit on trade and capital account. The Labor government was forced, after a long period of hesitation and half measures which made things worse, to institute a policy of retrenchment, exactly the opposite of what their spokesmen had been preaching for years and years when they were in opposition. The success of the policy of restraint is not yet assured. But the mild stagnation which it has produced is real enough.

With fixed exchanges, rigid wages, and a strong wage push, it is unavoidable that a country now and then gets into a situation where it has to choose between stifling exchange control or a higher level of unemployment and slower growth than it likes. A regime of flexible exchanges would bypass or at least alleviate these disagreeable dilemmas. But flexible exchanges cannot eliminate the possible conflict between the target of maximum long-run growth and continuously high level of employment. Nor are flexible exchange rates a cure for inflation.

Professor Allan H. Meltzer

Gottfried, as long as I can remember, people have been saying monetary policy could do better. Indeed, it could. Why doesn't it? And how many errors must it make before we all become convinced that some control on discretion is required, even if we don't adopt a fall rule?

If Professor Musgrave had not stated his position so clearly, my task would be more difficult; our disagreements would be less obvious and I would be left in the position of the discussant who must reply by saying: "Yes, but. . . ." Fortunately Musgrave has put forward a clear and able statement of his views —views that are shared by many others in the academic profession and are so widely held within the government that an alternative view is hard to find there. At one point in his paper Musgrave notes that the late Eisenhower and the early Kennedy Administrations advocated the same mix of policies to achieve growth and stability. Apparently there is the beginning of a political consensus that social problems can and will be solved only if we give a more active role to *ad hoc* government policies.

In view of the frankness, clarity, and ability—with which Professor Musgrave has advanced his views and argued his case, I can do no less than try to reciprocate. The disagreement between us, while not complete, is so large, that the area of agreement is insignificant in comparison. Moreover, the sources of our disagreement are, I believe, equally clear and equally obvious. Professor Musgrave and I reach different conclusions when we examine historical evidence. We disagree about who is responsible for choosing the goals of society. We place a different value on the importance of economic freedom; that is, we do not agree about the relative importance that should be placed on private and governmental decisions in the allocation of resources. I believe these matters are all related and that they are mainly the result of using different theories and, therefore, interpreting facts differently. Let me, therefore, state what I regard as the basis for the disagreements between us and illustrate our different approaches by reference to some of the points made in Professor Musgrave's paper. Then I shall argue, briefly, why I believe that the evidence largely supports the less popular alternative view and suggest that the very policies that Professor Musgrave advocates are a main cause of the worldwide failure to achieve full employment of resources without inflation and a main source of the fluctuations in economic activity that he and I desire to avoid.

Fortunately, my job has been made easier by the paper that was presented this morning. As I read Musgrave's paper, time and again I was struck by the difference in our approach. Each time he reached a point at which he thought a choice must be made between consumption and investment, between growth and balance-of-payments equilibrium, between public and private investment, he argued for some form of selective control, some new or renewed action by government. The fact that relative prices would change and that the market would express the public's preference for one or the other of these outcomes plays little or no role in his analysis. In fact, he goes much farther. If private decisions reflected in relative price changes threaten to interfere with society's "growth target," the government should introduce selective tax incentives to encourage investment. If monetary and fiscal policies cannot achieve the target rate of unemployment and price change because of administered prices, wage-price guidelines or income policies should be used. If the objectives of domestic policy conflict with the aims of our balance of payments, "selective controls can be constructed to deal with the situation." In short, as I read these rather popular suggestions, there is some combination of selective and general control that will achieve all of our objectives. If not, we invent more selective controls.

Whose objectives are to be achieved? Society's objectives as determined on the basis of a consensus within the executive agencies of government or within the Council of Economic Advisers or society's objectives as expressed in the marketplace? What has happened to our objective of maintaining a large measure of economic freedom, for example, as expressed in the right to register preferences for and against growth, or other goals and priorities selected by government by voting for an alternative allocation of resources in the marketplace?

At first glance, the answers to the questions I have just raised appear to depend on values, and doubtless there is an element of value judgment present. But I believe it is misleading to view the different answers that Professor Musgrave and I would be likely to give to the above questions as solely the result of different value systems. There is a clearcut difference in our approach to problems that should not be discussed or dismissed as a reflection of different goals for society. I am confident that Professor Musgrave, and many others who reach conclusions similar to his, would not wish to be cast as enemies of economic freedom, and I do not want to force them into that mold.

The difference between us is based mainly on the way in which we interpret facts, on the theories that we use and not on our goals. You may judge for yourself who is right by asking which of the interpretations fits the facts best. Is it true, as is so often claimed, that to achieve the many goals that are described in Musgrave's paper requires more or less continuous adjustment of monetary and fiscal policies and a variety of selective controls, as he says? Or, am I correct when I assert that the controls imposed by government and the almost continuous adjustment of monetary and fiscal policies make an important contribution to both inflation and unemployment and thus interfere with the economic system's efforts to secure stable growth, stable prices, and full use of resources? Is the popular view correct when it urges selective controls, wage-price guideposts, restrictions on foreign capital movements, and a variety of other *ad hoc* devices as a means of achieving frequently stated goals? Or am I correct when I argue that in most cases these selective devices are a source of instability that introduce uncertainty and hinder or prevent the economy from achieving many of the goals simultaneously?

The recent record of the U.S. economy provides excellent evidence with which to discriminate between these alternative views. Many of the controls that Musgrave and others desire to impose have been in effect during the past several years. For example, to control the balance of payments and to reduce the gold outflow, we have used a variety of formal and informal selective controls. To encourage growth in investment and capital goods, we have used tax credits and accelerated depreciation. To make inflation less apparent, we have relied upon that informal method of price control known as the wage-price guideposts, meanwhile adjuring repeatedly that wage and price controls are to be avoided. Despite these efforts, and I would say because of them, we have not maintained steady growth in employment, prevented inflation or balanced our international accounts without a gold outflow, although Presidents, congressmen, and secretaries of the Treasury have affirmed their allegiance to the present set of fixed exchange rates, they have used selective taxes and controls to change the exchange rate for particular types of transactions.

On one interpretation our main reason that production has fallen, that growth is slow, that inflation has returned and that the gold outflow persists and increases is that the government did not have enough selective controls. On the other interpretation, my interpretation, a main reason that we have not achieved these goals of policy is because the government's monetary and fiscal policies prevented us from doing so. As I view the record, it seems unmistakably clear that the very policies that Musgrave and many others now advocate have been tried repeatedly and have failed just as often.

Let me present some recent evidence to support my position more fully. During late 1965 and early 1966 when prices were rising, government officials either argued that there would be no inflation or urged unions and corporations to exercise restraint. As always at the start of inflation, the government either attempted to shift the responsibility for the inflation to the private sector or denied that the rise in prices was more than a temporary disturbance that would soon abate. When the Federal Reserve raised the discount rate in December, 1965, many officials and economists, within and outside government, deplored the lack of policy coordination but ignored the extremely high rate of increase in the stock of money. The rise in the discount rate was a mild anti-inflationary action, entirely too modest to offset the rate at which the Federal Reserve increased the money supply. Moreover, during the winter of 1966, the Federal Reserve increased the rate of increase of the money supply and added to the inflationary pressures.

On my interpretation a rate of increase in the money supply of 6 percent per annum is an inflationary rate of increase in money supply and is certainly an "easy policy."

Inflation is always the result of a sustained policy of monetary expansion. Contrary to popular opinion, inflation is not produced by monopolies in labor or in business, by speculators, housewives, farmers, middlemen, or by many of the other groups that are so frequently blamed. It is the result of government, not private policies, and particularly of government monetary policies. The inflation of 1966-67 does not differ in this regard from the inflations that we have had in the past or from the inflations that we are likely to have in the future. It does not differ from the inflations experienced in other countries. The 1966-67 inflation is (or will be) the result of government policy and particularly of the central bank's monetary policy.

Through most of the first six months of 1966 the Federal Reserve actively fed the inflation. The growth rate of the money supply, currency, and demand deposits rose to approximately 6 percent per annum, about twice the rate of increase that was desirable under the circumstances. In the summer of 1966 the Federal Reserve suddenly reversed its policy. The growth rate of the money supply fell. Then the money supply fell. Within a very few months monetary policy had switched from highly inflationary to highly contractive. It remained highly contractive until late in December, 1966, when it again reversed direction and suddenly became too expansive to be characterized as non-inflationary.

These wide swings in the direction of monetary policy were accompanied by smaller but nonetheless important changes in the expansive influence of fiscal policy. On my interpretation, the government's monetary and fiscal policies produced the inflation of 1966-67 and the very large changes in the size and direction of monetary policy produced the decline in industrial production, the reduction in employment, and in the growth rate of output. The present high rate of monetary expansion and the very large and very sharp change in the rate of change of money mean that more inflation is to be expected.

Furthermore, on my interpretation, the government's policies are the principal reason that we will not achieve full use of resources without inflation in 1967 and that we will continue to experience a gold outflow. The inflationary policies that the government pursued in late 1965 and early 1966 and that the government now is pursuing make our exports relatively more expensive and our imports relatively cheaper and thus move us away from balance-of-payments equilibrium. The system of exchange controls and special taxes does not—indeed cannot—bring about permanent adjustment of the balance of payments without a gold loss. At best, these controls give policymakers time in which to adjust the balance of payments at the present fixed exchange rate by pursuing policies that are less inflationary than those pursued in other countries. But in recent years, the United States has pursued inflationary policies and has not made wise use of the time purchased with direct controls and special taxes on foreign transactions.

The government's policies in 1966 likewise provide a main reason why output has grown very slowly and why industrial production has fallen in the first quarter of 1967. I have already indicated that the monetary and fiscal policies were inflationary until late spring or early summer. Once the Federal Reserve reversed its direction and forced the stock of money to decline, it was to be expected that industrial production would decline and that unemployment would increase.

The reason is that no anti-inflationary monetary policy can

succeed in stopping inflation unless it first has an effect on production and employment. Or, to put the point in another way, the effect of monetary policy on output is a part of the process by which monetary policy affects the price level and produces inflation, deflation, or price stability. The recent experience of the United States is by no means an isolated example. The policy that the British call Stop-and-Go is of the same kind and produced the same type of results, and these are not the only examples, of course.

The very policies that Professor Musgrave and others so often advocate, in my judgment, are the main cause of their failure to achieve their goals. The patchwork of direct controls, the extreme variability of monetary and fiscal operations, the exhortations that become threats and that are followed by laws, these, and not the absence of sufficient power, head the list of reasons that we and others fail to maintain full use of resources without inflation.

Finally, I would like to add that in a more complete discussion of the subject than I have been able to present it would be worthwhile considering two other points that neither Musgrave nor I mentioned. One of these is the activities in which the government now engages and some of the rules that are now enforced at all levels of government. Many of these rules create monopolies that reduce the level of employment that will be maintained at a zero rate of change of prices.

A second problem is the choice of goals and particularly the rough measure of equality that is often given to each of the goals. I find it difficult to understand how the maintenance of fixed exchange rates ever became a matter of the same importance as high employment and price stability. In fact, like Professor Harriss, I must confess my lack of conviction that fixed exchange rates are desirable. But these matters are best left to another session or to those who have allowed themselves more space to discuss Professor Harriss' thoughtful paper.

Professor Carl Shoup

Let me start by making just a few points with respect to Professor Harriss' paper. I would agree that the federal government's activity should serve everyone since everyone pays, but I think perhaps Professor Harriss might also agree with me that not every single action has to affect everyone. There is, after all, a respectable tradeoff that we can operate over time. I therefore question whether a general tax reduction is, even in the present circumstances, better than some increase in expenditure, or a refusal to decrease expenditure.

But be that as it may, we can agree that better data are needed. We are a rich enough country to have better data. We are a rich enough country so that we should by now have had several econometric models of very large scale, all having been tested for many years.

Finally, one other point. If the poor are to be helped, as all of us trust they will be, the help will have to come in large part from the middle-income classes and even to some extent from those who not long ago were in the poverty class themselves. From the political point of view, this is going to be one of the things that will make it rather more difficult to achieve than many of us would like.

Although the "numbers game," as Professor Musgrave puts it, can be overplayed, it is useful to keep thinking in terms of numbers of instruments and targets, and noting which instruments and which targets are, and which are not, independent of each other. To do so requires us to ask just how many different targets we are aiming at, and, if that number seems upon examination to be depressingly large, whether the number of instruments that we are choosing among may not in fact be larger than we realize.

The number of targets, for this purpose, depends partly on whether some of the goals we want to achieve are so linked that if one is reached the others are automatically reached. In that event, the bundle of goals make up one target. This point is illustrated in Professor Musgrave's opening pages, where the three goals of (1) high employment, (2) full resource [capital goods?] utilization, and (3) stable price level are lumped under the one target of "stabilization." The other target is rate of growth, or, more specifically, rate of investment. The two instruments are fiscal policy—change in tax yield or in government expenditure level at a given level of total output—and monetary policy—change in pattern or amount of money, or non-money claims against the government.

In the simplest case, where Target I (stabilization) is achievable only by Instrument I (fiscal policy) and Target II (growth) only by Instrument II (monetary policy), "the proper blend is determined unambiguously." But we may emphasize that the proper blend is also determined just as unambiguously when each of the two instruments affects the movement toward each of the two targets.

Trouble arises if one of the instruments turns out not to be effective in moving toward either target, as where "investment does not respond sufficiently to monetary ease" (Instrument II is not helpful in reaching either Target I or Target II). Then, "general policies become inadequate and selective tax devices such as the investment credit . . ." may be used. But this seems to me to be the same thing as saying that what we had tentatively identified as one instrument (fiscal policy) turns out to be a bundle of instruments. Accordingly, even if investment does "respond sufficiently to monetary ease" so that we do not search for a "selective" tax device, we must realize that a "general" tax change is made up of a number of particular tax changes, at least some of which, evidently may influence investment. In other words we are not really free to think that we are using just one instrument so long as we are having no trouble with "the" other instrument. Even a uniform percentage increase in personal income taxes alone must probably be regarded as a collection—for purposes of this particular two-target case—of at least two instruments, one, a tax on persons who neither save nor dissave, and another, a tax on those who do.

Nor is "monetary policy" really a one-instrument concept, especially if it includes debt management, but also if it does not. There are many different ways of achieving a given interest rate, but, more to the point, there are many interest rates. What we end up with is, even under the most simplifying assumptions, a considerable number of instruments, most of which affect both of the goals of stability and growth. With so many instruments relative to the number of targets, there is no longer an unambiguous proper blend of monetary and fiscal policy. There are many alternative combinations, depending on the internal pattern of the fiscal policy measure and on the internal pattern of the monetary measure.

If there were a useful concept of "a" truly "general" fiscal policy measure, the internal pattern of which would be defined sufficiently by the term "general" (implying, perhaps, "uniform" or "equal" or something like that), the distinction between "general" and "selective" measures would be useful. But the purpose of these remarks is to question whether such a distinction is really feasible. The difference between (1) changing the federal personal income tax and corporation income tax rates by a uniform percentage (and not changing the federal excise taxes, or payroll taxes, not to mention the various state and local taxes) and (2) changing the federal income tax by inserting tax relief for amounts spent on investment goods, but not changing any other part of the income tax, is a difference in degree only. And the "general" change itself really consists of a host of "special" changes, the pattern of which is not defined by the word "general."

But happily this embarrassment of riches in number of instruments turns out to be a necessity rather than an embarrassment, for two reasons.

First, use of a fiscal policy instrument implies also the use of one of the monetary instruments, save in rare instances. Few would advocate only balanced-budget changes in taxation and spending as instruments of policy. And a mere change in pattern of taxation, with no change in yield, or in pattern of spending, is also likely to be an awkward instrument. Accordingly, in practice a decision to grant an investment credit, for example, is also an implicit decision to sell more government debt or create more money. Instead of achievement of one target now implying achievement of another, which makes life easier, the use of one instrument now implies concomitant use of another, and this makes achievement of the targets more difficult.

Second, it also turns out, as suggested earlier, that what may at first seem to be one target is really a number of targets that are not automatically achieved together, as Professor Musgrave points out clearly. Not only does stabilization break down into high employment, full resource utilization, and a stable price level, but other targets aside from growth demand attention, notably external equilibrium. And if we still have an excess of instruments, there are plenty of inviting targets lying around, even in addition to those mentioned by Professor Musgrave (fiscal discipline and income distribution): reduction of excess burden, maintenance of a desired level of governmental decentralization in a federal nation, and so on.

One reason, I am inclined to believe, why so little progress has been made in practice toward achieving a proper blend of fiscal and monetary policy is that whenever an attempt is made to formulate a specific program, all the considerations I have mentioned crowd in upon us, demanding attention; we become aware that there are not two instruments and two targets, indeed we intuitively realize that there is no one "general" instrument in the sense that the discussants know just what each other is talking about when they speak of a "general" instrument. Discussion becomes confused and planning becomes vague or at the other extreme, lost in detail.

Yet of course we cannot carry on a discussion in terms of say 100 instruments and 100 targets. Probably the next step is largely to abandon the attempt to reach a proper mix of fiscal policy and monetary policy, now that this question has served to start us on the road, and to break these "two" policies down into, say, five instruments, with an equivalent number of independent targets, and to assume initially that each instrument affects movement toward each target. Time would then tell whether this framework can lead to a policy prescription that is precise enough to stimulate action, yet not so detailed as to paralyze thought.

The initial assumption that any one of the instruments will affect the approach toward any one of the targets is a safeguard in alerting us to results that we might otherwise overlook, although they are perfectly deducible a priori. Two striking examples come to mind from 1966, when two fiscal policy measures had the effect usually attributed only to monetary measures, of tightening the money market, causing a rise in interest rates. One was the provision that speeded up corporate tax payments, putting large corporations more quickly on a completely current payment basis. More tax revenue was brought in during the year, but partly by the creation of new money, as some corporations went to the banking system for funds to pay the accelerated tax. The other measure was the suspension of the investment credit. Anticipation of the suspension caused a wave of orders, with consequent repercussions on the hiring and purchasing schedules of the vendee firms in the machinery and allied industries, and, by inference, on their borrowings.

Another good example of this same general thesis is supplied by Professor Musgrave's reminder that the instrument of monetary policy affects our movement toward a target that is traditionally thought to be pursuable only by fiscal policy, namely, a certain distribution of income, and I am inclined to agree with him that substitution of general credit restraint for the type of tax restraint he defines would be regressive— provided we define "general" more closely.

Among the targets discussed by Professor Musgrave is one that may not be a target at all in the same sense that full employment, price stability, and external equilibrium are targets; I refer to fiscal discipline. It is, of course, almost by definition desirable, but it is an objective directly attainable, also by definition, through fiscal measures; it is, in fact, what fiscal measures are about whereas full employment and the like are desiderata to be attained by the proper choice among countless sets of fiscal measures all of which reflect fiscal discipline— the reasoned choice of a certain proportion of the nation's output to be in the form of public goods. If the economic environment is such that full employment can only be maintained, without inflation or external disequilibrium, by a continual deficit, fiscal discipline does not, of course, call for a balanced budget. When unemployment appears, the unemployed resources are really free resources, for either public use or private use, and neither fiscal discipline nor private-market discipline should, rationally, force anyone to give up something in order to get more private or public goods. The ratio in which this increment of temporarily free goods should be divided between public and private goods is not a discipline matter, whatever else it is.

One final word on the usefulness of the distinction between fiscal and monetary policy. I think these terms are still useful. What I am suggesting is that general fiscal policy and general monetary policy have little, if any, real meaning. But it is still useful to ask whether a particular measure goes into the box called measures of fiscal policy or into another box called measures of monetary policy. Fiscal policy measures involve coercion, legal coercion; we ask somebody to do something that he doesn't want to do. Or the coercion is negative, in the case of tax reduction. Measures of monetary policy are those that operate through the market, on a voluntary or at least quasi-voluntary basis.

This may be the reason why we find it so difficult to get executive discretion allowed for fiscal policy. Parliaments and legislatures like to keep coercive measures in their own hands, while they are willing to delegate to the executive those measures that operate through the market on a voluntary basis.

If this is so, it probably follows that, because the executive can act more quickly than the legislature, monetary policy measures will tend to be employed earlier than fiscal policy measures.

Mr. Norman B. Ture

I have organized my discussion on a first-in, first-out basis and because Professor Musgrave's paper reached me ahead of Professor Harriss', I deal somewhat more extensively with the former than with the latter. This also accounts for the title of my discussion: The Fiscal-Monetary Policy Mixup.

Professor Musgrave has given us what may prove to be the definitive discussion of the blend or mix of fiscal and monetary policies. He neatly lines up the policy objectives, delineates clearly the issues and problems to be encountered, sets out the solutions and, in the best tradition of scholarship, concludes with some cautions about the validity of the analysis. Let us all hope that this is indeed the definitive discussion so that we can turn our attention to matters of greater import in the field of political economy. Particularly let us hope that Professor Musgrave can reallocate his redoubtable intellectual resources to more consequential lines of activity.

Of course, the efficiency with which resources are allocated among their alternative uses does not appear to be a major concern of public economic policy these days. Possibly this is attributable to the ascendancy of the new economics, the primary interest of which is in the policy goals of full employment and economic growth. It isn't, however, this focus which distinguishes new economists from not-so-new economists or even very old economists but rather their deep conviction that they have found the answers to the achievements of these goals. New economists, thus, speak of targets—target unemployment rates and target growth rates, among others—and they let it be known that they know how to hit the bull's-eye. Failure to do so, it turns out, is the fault of the institutions with which public economic policy is encumbered; if only fiscal policy changes could be effected without having to deal with the untutored, ill-advised, misdirected Congress—if only the President could do it all by himself, under the guidance, of course, of his educated, insightful, properly oriented economic advisers.

Professor Musgrave, it is clear from his concluding remarks, is not to be included among these new economists, since he avows at the end of his paper, that, "The uncertainty of economic change and the difficulty of predicting lags as well as magnitudes in the responses to various policies make it exceedingly difficult to accomplish a set of interacting objectives." Until that point in his discussion, however, he had us fooled.

Lest these remarks on the new economics be construed as digressing from the original observation that hopefully, with Professor Musgrave's remarks, we will be done with the question of the "policy mix," consider that the policy mix argument is what principally separates new economists from all others. The hallmark of the new economics is the system of notions that there is at any particular time some right combination of monetary ease or constraint and fiscal constraint or ease which will control the short-run rate of growth of aggregate demand, hence, the rate of resource utilization, and the rate of expansion of production capability. The neatness of this analytical structure is wonderfully appealing to new economists, whose passion for activism is or would be unbearably strained by a public policy approach which relied on underplaying public intervention in society's economic affairs and was content with minimizing the economic shocks generated by public actions. So, for example, new economists insist on alertness to changing economic conditions and frequent changes in taxes and/or expenditures, and/or interest rates, which, incidentally, they construe to mean monetary policy. They abhor such prescriptions as those which call for a smooth rate of expansion of the money supply or those which imply a diffident view about the need for utility in accelerating or retarding public expenditure programs or those which call for a stable tax environment on which consumers and investors alike may rely in planning their economic activities.

What surely is puzzling is the ready acceptance of notions as untested as the policy mix. This is, after all, an era of empiricism—everything gets run through the computer before its validity is accepted or rejected. Yet it is difficult to see how any machine, other than one having a nervous breakdown, could validate some of the basic premises of the policy mix argument.

One of these premises, for example, is that increases in taxes relative to government expenditures will curb the expansion of aggregate demand, while the reverse budgetary development will stimulate GNP expansion. In the new economics, this is slightly elaborated to eliminate the confusion between endogenous changes in government receipts and expenditures and those resulting from discretionary changes in policy; thus, it is the change in the full-employment surplus (or deficit), that is to say, the excess or short fall of receipts over expenditures which would result at "full" employment, that affects the rate of expansion of aggregate demand. Professor Musgrave's discussion brings this critical assumption clearly into the open, for which we must be grateful to him.

He asserts that it can hardly be doubted and will stand that higher taxes will deter consumption. But it surely may be doubted both on theoretical and empirical grounds that there is a reliable functional relationship between changes in disposable income and changes in consumption in the short run. Indeed, the whole notion that changes in national income are functionally related to changes in autonomous expenditures has been contested vigorously in the recent scholarly literature.

We may not have the final score but, at the least, it is clear that Professors Friedman and Meiselman have not fled in disorder and confusion from the counterattacks of Professors Ando, Modigliani, DePrano, and Mayer, nor have Professors Meltzer and Brunner. The validity of the contention that changes in the full-employment surplus affect the rate of expansion of aggregate demand is at issue in this conflict of analytical systems. If the contention is rejected or held to be of unproved validity, the whole analytical structure linking fiscal policy changes directly to changes in the rate of expansion of aggregate demand falls apart. And if it does so, then the concern with the fiscal-monetary policy mix as determining simultaneously the rate of expansion of aggregate demand and the growth rate is inconsequential.

Perhaps the least demanding test the full-employment surplus thesis should be asked to pass is that changes in the rate of change of gross national product should be of opposite sign to changes in the full-employment surplus. Beginning with the first quarter of 1948 and continuing through the last quarter of 1966, the signs of the respective changes the same —therefore wrong—in 37 of the 74 quarterly observations. If the change in the rate of change of GNP is lagged four quarters behind the change in the full-employment surplus, the sign changes are the same—wrong—in 36 out of 71 cases. With a three quarter lag, the sign changes are wrong in 41 out of 72 cases. With a two quarter lag, the test is failed in 42 of 73 cases, and for a single quarter lag, in 42 of 74 cases.

While such tests are not definitive, it is hard to understand how any objective analysis could find in the data a reliable relationship between changes in fiscal parameters and the national income. Example can be piled upon example but I will cite only one.

Between the first and last quarters of 1948 the full-employment surplus fell by something like the order of magnitude of $14 billion but, as you all know, this did not forefend the recession in the late fall of that year.

The basic premise of fiscal policy thus appears to emerge as an article of faith, which however beautiful as an abstraction is a shaky foundation upon which to base policy. Thus, one can only be dismayed by the proposal by the highest high priest of the new economics for substantial tax increases this year aimed only at validating an easier monetary policy. In this instance, incidentally, the objective in changing the policy mix is not to promote faster growth in the capital stock—as one might surmise from Professor Musgrave's discussion; it is, rather, to ease the financial pressure on the residential construction industry. In short, according to this proposal, the entire economy would bear a 6 percent tax as surcharge for the benefit of an industrial sector which in 1966 accounted for scarcely $3\frac{1}{3}$ percent of gross national product. In fairness to Professor Musgrave, it should be emphasized that he expresses some reservations on this score; his preference is for selective measures to rescue housing.

Professor Musgrave is not blind to certain other analytical constraints on the operational validity of the policy mix proposition. Thus, he poses the possibility that investment is unresponsive to changes in interest rates or that changes in credit terms may influence major components of consumption so that general monetary measures may be ineffectual in influencing the volume of investment and may have unwanted effects on consumption. Professor Musgrave is not daunted; selective fiscal and monetary measures come to the rescue. Apart from the improbability that the income or price effects of selective measures can be effective when the same sort of income and price effects of more general measures are presumed to be inoperative, selective measures are almost certainly worse in consequence than the difficulties at which they are directed.

In the same vein Professor Musgrave raises the objection to the general policy mix propositions that the problems of economic instability may not be one of excess demand but may arise from "cost push." Here, wage-price guideposts presumably rescue us from the dilemma of the Phillips curve. Having seen them in operation, however, we should be under no illusion that wage-price guideposts are anything other than the cover under which the political authorities attempt to control the prices of those industries which are more than ordinarily concerned with their public relations; in other words, wage-price guidelines are selective controls, a point which Professor Samuelson, incidentally, has recently emphasized.

Professor Musgrave also deals with some constraints on the determination of the particular policy mix which will assure an expansion of aggregate demand in line with potential aggregate output, the short-run stabilization problem. These constraints are both analytical and institutional in nature. In the former case, he asserts that private consumption and investment functions are unstable but this instability apparently only gives rise in his view to the need for frequent policy changes. But if indeed private spending functions do change frequently and unsystematically, we shall never be able to anticipate the changes in private spending in time to offset them, even if we had the public policy devices with which to do so. For if we were able to forecast these changes, it would only be because they occurred in some systematic way, in which case there would be no problem of the sort Professor Musgrave cites.

The second set of constraints adduced by Professor Musgrave are institutional—the policy lags, three of which he identifies: (1) recognition, (2) action, (3) effectiveness. He dismisses the recognition lag, that is, the period elapsing between the time that forces generating an economic disturbance go into operation and the time the disturbance is recognized. He dismisses that lag as applying equally in the case of fiscal and monetary policy changes and therefore not relevant to the question of policy mix. But surely this is a non sequitor, since if this lag is long and the disturbance is relatively short, the chances of successful use of any discretionary, compensatory policies are remote. It is not a matter of mix but of whether any kind of stabilization policy is workable with a substantial recognition lag.

The second lag is the one on which new economists always focus their attack by insisting that Congress is to blame for tardy fiscal policy changes and should be excluded from the process. The third lag, the time it takes for a policy change to affect business and consumer behavior, in the case of the fiscal policy is deemed to be very short, although I must say the evidence for this view is, as I have indicated, very thin. Monetary policy, on the other hand, is thought to be slow acting. It is really academic, however, whether the second and third lags are long or short, since in the postwar period the first lag has been so substantial as effectively to preclude the successful use of an anticyclical fiscal or monetary policy or any mix thereof.

It is tempting to continue to dip into the rich stew that Professor Musgrave has served up but there is another course on the menu.

Professor Harriss sets himself the task of categorizing the objectives of fiscal and budget policies and identifies these as full employment, avoidance of inflation, equity in the distribution of the burdens and benefits (of public policies), economic growth, and effective participation in world economy. While not explicitly citing them as separate objectives, his discussion also implicitly places great weight on efficiency and economic freedom as part of the inventory of public policy goals.

Public policy has indeed been concerned with these matters in the current era, but the pertinent issue for this discussion is not whether, as a society, we have paid attention to them, but rather how these goals can be usefully framed and what collectively we can or should do about them.

In the first connection, it would be wonderfully useful if we could agree, all of us henceforth, to speak of these goals only in ordinal rather than in cardinal terms. How rapidly should the per capita production capability of the economy expand? Other things equal, more rapidly. How low should the rate of unemployment be? Lower. How equal a distribution of income and wealth should be sought? Less unequal. How rapidly should the general level of prices rise? Less rapidly, and so forth. The point of such restatements of public policy concerns, of course, is to emphasize that there are no absolutes for policy purposes and the concepts of stability, growth, equity, freedom and that we merely spin our wheels in arguing such points. Thus, for example, there is little to be gained from explaining why inflation should be avoided. The issue never arises in this form in any case and if it were to, with no other goals of public policy involved, it would in any event be moot. It is only because doing something which may affect the rate at which the general level of prices advances in a particular period of time may have some repercussions on how the economy performs against other criteria that an issue arises and that there is a public concern with maintaining price-level stability.

In the second case, the mere fact that there is a collective interest which can be generalized as a goal of society need not imply that the goal is best achieved or achieved at all— through public action. It does not follow from the fact that we are, as a nation, concerned with the pace of our economic growth that there is some particular set of fiscal devices that we should use to this end. Nor does the mere fact of our concern with the price level and the rate of use of our production capabilities necessarily cast up a prescription for current public policies in these connections.

This is, we must concede, an era of activism, particularly in our public life. Apparently it does not do merely to identify or describe a problem, one must as well afford the solution to it and be up and at it. We have had quite a few months of agitation in fiscal and monetary policies. Is it too much to hope that the irrelevance, at best, or the mischief, at worst, of all of the stirring about will eventually become sufficiently apparent to abate the fervor for a "flexible" fiscal and monetary policy?

Discussion and Questions from the Floor

Professor Musgrave: Let me start with Professor Meltzer and a word about the nature of our disagreement. There are two questions here. One is values on which one can specify one's position and then agree to differ; the other is a question of how the economy actually works. Here he and I may be interested in testing different hypotheses, but in the end both would be willing to be persuaded if the evidence is there.

On the matter of values, there is to begin with the question, as he put it, of how does one value freedom as against other things? But there is a real problem in defining "freedom." Our interpretation of the term may not be the same. Do we mean F.D.R.'s four freedoms, or freedoms, or noninterference with the marketplace? The latter may help the former, but the two are not the same. I want freedom just as much as Dr. Meltzer, but I suspect that we mean different things by it.

But suppose we agree on how individual freedom is to be defined as a goal. People really don't differ very much on this in American society, that's why it works. Then there is another matter of values, which may be more relevant to our disagreement. You see, nature could be such that in order to realize the agreed-on freedom, a great deal of social cooperation is needed; or, nature may be such, as in a Thomas Aquinas' world, that things take care of themselves. Maybe you have to install a built-in formula once, but then the natural order functions all right. Some people would like to wake up in the morning and find nature such that a lot of cooperation is required to make things work; and others would like to wake up and find nature such that freedom can be realized without much cooperation. This is really where value judgments and temperaments differ most, and where political debate is needed.

Leaving values, and turning to the objective facts, we now deal with problems on which science must eventually rule. The answer must be given by factual findings. The basic difference lies in how we see the nature of the macrosystem to work. While we could write down a formulation which is so broad as to command general acceptance, when we get more specific we begin to disagree. This goes for both targets and policies.

Regarding targets, if one postulates a wholly flexible macrosystem, one might say growth is not a policy target because the market may be relied on to determine the growth rate in relation to time preferences of savers. If one postulates what I consider a more realistic system with various kinds of rigidities, the system itself will not produce an optimal growth rate and growth becomes a matter of public policy. I think it is, and Professor Meltzer probably doesn't.

Similarly, different policies will do different things, depending on the nature of the macrosystem which we postulate. Dr. Meltzer and I differ in our evaluation of monetary and fiscal measures. Also, we may differ in the extent to which our present institutional environment can be changed. Can we break up Ford and General Motors, together with the UAW and the international unions, and establish flexible markets in which stabilization policy would take care of itself? I don't think we can, but we might differ on that.

We also differ, I think, on how well we have done. Dr. Meltzer feels that we have done very poorly. I think by and large, that during the 1960s we have done pretty well. In all, there are too many points of disagreement to consider in detail. I feel that I have presented a rather balanced view of the problem, but it will be for you to judge. I might add that Professor Meltzer will be at Harvard next year. The graduate students will listen to him in the first semester and to Professor Tobin in the second, and all we will have to do is to ask them in the generals to find out who was right.

Turning to Professor Haberler's comments, let me correct what I said about the sine curve. What I meant is that people used to talk about a curve wiggling around a horizontal line, but that we are in fact dealing with a curve wiggling around an upward trend. This being the case, the downward phase may involve merely a slower rate of increase, but not an absolute decline.

On the matter of the tax increase, I don't quite see how Professor Haberler knows that the President did not want to recommend it; he may have better inside information, but I believe that such a recommendation would have been made had the Congress been more willing. And I find Mr. Mills' statement of last night most distressing. On the matter of the investment credit, Professor Haberler is right in noting that such changes take quite awhile to become effective. They cannot be used in the short-run cyclical context, and much depends on how long the periods are over which you have to restrict and expand. If they are two quarters, it's one thing. If they are a year or two, it's another. Last year's experience falls in between, but lacking the possibility of increasing income taxes, it was probably correct to suspend the credit. In any case, if we argue that changing the investment credit doesn't work in the short-run situation because the lag is too long, the same thing holds for the effects of monetary policy, at least those which operate on plant and equipment expenditures. But if this is the case and the short-run monetary effect is limited to housing, why not have an excise tax on housing starts instead?

As to the 1959 episode, it happens that the mistake was made by Republicans, but whoever made it, I think that it was not excusable. There should have been ways of dealing with the balance-of-payments problem, other than creating a repression, especially since private capital outflow remained high in 1959, notwithstanding the restrictive monetary measures. Surely, the price that was paid was too high. More generally, I agree that high employment is not a remedy to the balance-of-payments situation. In the early 1960s it was argued by Secretary Dillon and others that high employment would be helpful on trade account, because it would speed technological progress and business would be able to sell more cheaply. But you probably lose more on imports than you gain on exports, and while effects on capital account will be favorable, they will hardly outweigh the trade effects. This does not mean that I favor holding down employment, but I would not sell high employment on balance-of-payments grounds.

I generally agree with Professor Shoup that the broad distinction between general monetary and general fiscal policy is insufficient, and that a finer set of distinctions is needed, along the lines which he suggests. He is also quite correct in pointing out that fiscal discipline as a target should be defined in marginal terms. The true economic discipline, of course, is to push public expenditures to the point where the marginal gain in the public sector is just offset by the marginal loss in the private sector. My concern, here, was rather with the political discipline of equity between taxes and expenditures. This again should be formulated in marginal terms, but the question is whether even then it can be made compatible with the needs of stabilization policy. I think that it can not, especially in the cyclical context.

Turning finally to Mr. Ture's points, I think he is wrong in holding that we should talk about targets such as growth, price stability, and employment in ordinal terms only without specifying how much. Since the achievement of targets involves costs, we must know how much we would accomplish; and since the cost may be in terms of conflicts with other targets, we must be able to consider tradeoffs between them. This we cannot do without a cardinal approach. Mr. Ture thinks of the issue of policy mix as being the essence of the new economics, so-called. If I have lent support to this impression, I should like to correct it. In fact, I don't care too much about this aspect, and was not too happy with the emphasis on it in the economic reports. I think the essence of the "new economics," or the (by now) 30-year-old economics, or in any case the right economics is that you can use it to maintain a reasonably high level of employment. That's primarily what it is about.

Professor Harriss: I have nothing, really to which to rejoin, but three brief points may be in order.

One: A question I raised seems to be worth a moment's thought: why growth becomes a matter of governmental policy as against the result of personal decision?

Second: With respect to the balance of payments, why pay

interest to hold gold? Why not let the gold leave, reduce our obligations, and save the cost of interest?

Third: The implicit assumption that a tax increase will reduce aggregate demand seems questionable because in view of the propensity of Congress and the executive to increase expenditures, any increase in revenues would probably be followed very quickly by an increase in government expenditures.

Mr. Ture: Dick, I don't understand why you assert in rejoinder that you think perhaps general income tax changes would have been preferable to suspension of the investment credit. If I recall that debate a few months ago with any kind of clarity at all, the objective was to curb plant and equipment orders, production, and expenditures in that sequence. If you feel that Gottfried is right in claiming that there is a long lag between the time that the suspension would be enacted to the time that you would actually see its effects in a decline in the rate of spending, what reason do you have to believe that a general tax change would have produced the effects any sooner?

Or would you rather have had a general tax change to curb private consumption? Nobody thought—as I recall, nobody was suggesting that we ought to curb consumption outlays because of this "unsustainable, excessive, inflation-generating" level of capital goods output.

I really raise this question with you, not actually to get an answer but only to emphasize the fact that I think this is an area in which the notion that you can use these fiscal devices to achieve specific objectives in the stabilization field is really one which strains credulity.

Professor Musgrave: My recommendation in early 1966, and I said so before the Joint Economic Committee, was that there should be an increase in income taxes to curtail consumption expenditures because this would be effective more promptly. The advantage of the much shorter lag would have more than offset the more selective but slower impact on capital expenditures.

Mr. Ture: A further reduction in automobile sales, and sales of television sets and other consumer durables—were they proceeding at an unsustainably inflationarily high rate? Or perhaps too many haircuts?

Professor Ira O. Scott, Long Island University: Professor Meltzer has relegated countercyclical monetary policy to the junkheap. Mr. Ture has done the same to fiscal policy. This leaves us, I take it, with a residual in the form of a secular policy of some sort, which is not a prospect that I regard with pleasure inasmuch, as we all know, "in the long-run we are all dead!"

However, I would like to put a question to Professor Meltzer. It is possible that the lags of monetary policy, which I am sure concern him, are providing the basis for a rationale of the Fed's "stop and go" policy. That is to say, is it not possible to move a given impact nearer the time by a more intense policy injection at the present time?

Professor Meltzer: This is as briefly as I will treat it. I believe there is substantial evidence which suggests, that the length of the lag, as well as its variability, depends upon the variability of policy operations.

To use a metaphor, and not a very good one, often we are not shooting at a moving target, but moving the target that we are shooting at. Consequently the main advantage of having some kind of stable policy is to avoid or reduce instability that is caused by the variations in policy.

What I am saying is that swings of the kind that we have had are too large. It seems to me unreasonable to expect that these large changes in policies do not have an impact, first on output, and later on prices.

So that when you look at the rates of change of output and prices, you do not know to what extent you are observing current effects, past effects, and how much of these effects are going to be damped or intensified because of the variability of past policy.

Professor John A. Menge, Dartmouth College: Just as Professor Meltzer thanked Professor Musgrave for being specific, I also would like to thank Professor Meltzer for being specific in his comment. Because if I hadn't heard it, I quite frankly wouldn't have believed it. I still don't. It seems to me

that what Professor Meltzer was saying was that essentially—
in fact, he so stated—prices, of course, determine the private
goals in the private market and they also determine the
governmental goals. And there are some I think who would
disagree with this, primarily the majority of the electorate.
I'm wondering just whose freedom we should infringe upon
in this instance.

Furthermore, if we do determine that the pricing system
does not determine all goals and objectives, then, of course, we
have to use some policies other than price policies. If we have
to use something other than price policy, then we can't simply
shrug off this problem as Norm Ture has done. We are going
to have to determine whether or not we're using good or bad
policy.

Professor Meltzer: Over what run? Over what run will the
rigidities persist? Professor Musgrave and I largely agree
that it is not a matter of goals and values. It is a matter of
judgments about what the world is like. Over what run will
the rigidities persist? Which rigidities are going to be the
hardest to remove? Will the policies and the ends that you
want to achieve by acting outside of the marketplace or by
improving new restrictions make society more or less adaptable
to change?

Is it the size of General Motors, as Professor Musgrave
apparently believes, or the laws of the City of New York
restricting the number of taxicabs that causes more unemployment among Negroes?

Is it the laws imposed by government regulatory agencies,
such as minimum wages, hours of work, licensing of barbers—
are those the things which are causing unemployment among
Negroes or which reduce the amount of employment that
society is going to have at a zero rate of change of prices?

Is it the monopoly elements—the monopolies maintained by
government—that cause the problem, or is it the pricing
behavior of private monopolists that is so often pointed to?

I believe it is the former, and I believe that the evidence is
very, very clear that we could reduce the unemployment rate
and raise the growth rate improving the efficiency of the
allocative mechanism and by removing the restrictions that
government imposes.

INDEX

213

216